Beyond Boundaries: The Future of World Research

EDITOR IN CHIEF
RHITURAJ SAIKIA

EDITORS
PRATISHA KUMARI

SUKHWINDER SINGH

SACHIN SURYAKANT MALI

RATAN BHATTACHARJEE

SREERAMA RAJASEKHAR

MEHEDI HASAN MANIK

SHANTHI IDA SOPHIA

BEATRIX BANKA

ANINDITA SANTRA

EDITORIAL

In an era defined by rapid technological advancements, complex global challenges, and unprecedented interconnectedness, the landscape of research is evolving at an extraordinary pace. "Beyond Boundaries: The Future of World Research" is a seminal work that captures this transformation, offering a comprehensive exploration of the future trajectories of global research.

This book emerges at a critical juncture, where the necessity for interdisciplinary collaboration and innovative thinking has never been more apparent. As Editor-in-Chief, Dr. Alexander Thompson, alongside a distinguished editorial board, has meticulously curated contributions from leading scholars across various fields to provide readers with an insightful and forward-thinking perspective on the future of research.

The title "Beyond Boundaries" encapsulates the core ethos of this book. It signifies the breaking down of traditional silos, encouraging a fusion of ideas, disciplines, and methodologies. In a world where problems are increasingly global and multifaceted, the need for research that transcends conventional boundaries is paramount.

ISBN:

CONTENTS

1.Issues and Concerns of the Day Care, Kindergarten and Grade 1 Teachers of Sulu in the Teaching of Literacy: A Causal Study

Dr. Rania D. Abduraup

Sulu State College, **Philippines**

Abstract: The significance of early literacy development in fostering academic success underscores the importance of evaluating the curriculum implemented in early education. This study investigates the issues and concerns faced by Day Care, Kindergarten, and Grade 1 teachers in Sulu Province regarding literacy instruction. Employing a descriptive quantitative research design, data were gathered from fifteen purposively sampled teachers, comprising five from each educational level. Findings reveal multifaceted challenges within three primary components: teaching strategies and readiness, pupils' readiness, and instructional support. Teachers encounter obstacles such as lack of pedagogical preparation, students' insufficient readiness and prior knowledge, and limited exposure to effective teaching strategies. Moreover, inadequate support from school administrators and stakeholders, coupled with limited financial resources, exacerbates instructional challenges. Furthermore, the study identifies deficiencies in pupils' readiness across various literacy domains, indicating gaps in phonemic awareness, vocabulary, fluency, and language comprehension. Notably, learners exhibit varied levels of preparedness, emphasizing the foundational role of early literacy skills in academic progression. Additionally, teachers express a collective need for enhanced training and support to address literacy instruction effectively. Recommendations include organizing seminars and supplemental trainings, conducting skills assessments for teachers, and implementing post-training evaluations to gauge progress. Continuous monitoring and evaluation, along with efforts to strengthen parental and stakeholder involvement, are proposed to enhance literacy initiatives. This study contributes insights for educational stakeholders to design targeted interventions and underscores the importance of ongoing professional development for educators in promoting early literacy proficiency. Future research is encouraged to expand the scope and population, thereby validating and extending these findings.

Keywords: causal comparative study, language education, literacy teaching, Philippines

Introduction

The development of early literacy is significant in preparing the pupils to accomplish academic success. The importance of early education in the learning and development of the child establishes a need to evaluate the curriculum implemented (Mann et al., 2022). Elementary schools commonly implement different teaching instructions and provide different materials without assessing whether the application of these methods will address the individual needs of the pupils (Kilag et al., 2022). The inability of preschool pupils to acquire the necessary literacy skills in reading will prevent them from achieving academic success in the elementary grade levels, in secondary and eventually in the college education (Phiri et al., 2024). This is mostly brought about by inappropriate teaching methods in the classrooms. There are studies done to evaluate the efficiency of the curriculum in developing early literacy development and readiness among primary pupils and preschoolers (Wilcox et al., 2020). There is experimental program that is designed to improve the reading and writing skills of pupils within preschool and primary age experiences. The teachers are optimistic that early literacy is vital in the development of every K to Grade 3 learners before they shall proceed grade 4 which is more on the content area of focus. The challenges faced by the teachers do not only consist of "what" (content) and "how" (pedagogy) to teach but also of the need to address the diversity of learners, the "who" of the teaching learning process (Morales et al., 2016). This is one of the reasons that the researcher chose this thesis problem because it is a national issue particularly it concerns education in which it is an effective tool to remedy illiteracy problems. It is a national issue because it poses challenges to the present system of education due to the enactment of Republic Act No. 10533 known as "Enhanced Basic Education Act of 2013." Education is a basic necessity of the individual person in the society. Educators have driven the Filipinos towards good education. Unfortunately, they do not possess quality of education. Meanwhile, traditional education is characterized by learning strategies such as memorization of facts and formula. This is perceived to have a growing irrelevance for the students of today. Conversely, progressive education is described to be child-centered, rather than textbook-centered, and grounded on authority (Hampel, 2008). The curiosity and creativity of students are highlighted by using strategies that would awaken a wide range of interests (Looi et al., 2023). Fortunately, the advent of K to 12 curriculum gave teachers a new hope to improve the quality of education brought forward by the new curriculum that could help the learners achieve better result in national assessment tests. For this, to ensure that the enhanced basic education program meets the demand for quality teachers and school leaders, the DepEd and the CHED, in collaboration with relevant partners in government, academe, industry, and nongovernment organization, shall conduct teacher education and training programs (RA 10533). Republic Act 10533 states that the current DepEd teachers shall be retrained to meet the content and performance standards of the K to 12 curricula. Likewise, the DepEd shall ensure that private education institution shall be given the opportunity to avail of such training. The K to 12 Basic Education Curriculum is a new program serves as the flagship educational programs of the Department of Education along with the strategies of teaching attuned to the 21st century skills. The K to 12 Education curriculum was launched effective school year 2012-2013 in all public elementary and secondary schools including the Private schools. The K to 12 curricula was assumed to further enhances to suit the school vision and mission (DepEd Order No. 31, s. 2012). The implementation is a must in public and private schools pursuant to the reform and thrust of the Basic Education Sector Reform Agenda, a package of policy reform that seeks to systematically improve the institutional, structural, financial, cultural, physical, and informational that affect basic education provision, access and delivery on the ground. "Give every student an opportunity to receive quality education that is globally competitive based on pedagogically sound curriculum that is par with international standards, and broaden the goals of high school education for college preparation,"(RA 10533) posed a great challenge to the present system of education. The challenges confronting the Department of Education are great but are not insurmountable. Education outcomes in terms of achievement, participation and completion rates point to the urgent need to improve the quality of basic education in the country. The National Achievement Test results for S.Y 2005-10 shows that many students who finished basic education in science do not possess sufficient mastery of basic competencies. In High school Science, it ranked 43rd out of 46 participating countries. In TIMMS or Trends in International Mathematics and Science Study, 2008 for advanced Math, the Philippines ranked 10th out of10 countries, (Mulis, et al., 2020). For the DepEd-ARMM Education Program continues to starve. According to UNESCO (As cited by Ladjakahal, et al.) Bangsamoro Autonomous Region in Muslim Mindanao had the highest "Educational Poverty" in the country which is at 14.8 % (or a percentage of those aged 17-22 years old with less than 4 years of education). On the Early Grade Reading Assessment conducted by the RTI (Research Triangle International) says, 55% of the Grade 2 Learners are not reading on reading on their level, 25% of which do not know the sounds of the Alphabet. This issue leads to non-reading because of the lack of knowledge on Phonics and Phonemic Awareness that is supposed to be leading to decoding and eventually recognizing of words. It is revealed too, that 59% of the learners have no reading materials being read at home, 15% have no access to books, Perhaps, the genuine love for reading is not a possibility at all.The desire to provide empirical data relating to the issues and concerns of the daycare, kindergarten and grade 1 teachers served as the motivating force for the conduct of this study.

Statement of the Problem

The main purpose of the study is to determine the Issues and Concerns of the Day Care, Kindergarten and Grade 1 Teachers of Sulu in the Teaching of Literacy. This study is also purposely done to bridge the gap between learners learning needs and teachers teaching approaches.

Specifically, it seeks to answer the following research questions:

1. What is the professional profile of Day Care, kinder and Grade 1 teachers of Sulu?

2. What are the issues and concerns of the Day Care, Kinder and Grade 1 Teachers of Sulu in teaching literacy in terms of?

    a. teaching Strategies and readiness

    b. pupils' Readiness

    c. instructional support

Literature Review: According to Durlak et al. (2022), school-based programs can positively impact a wide range of social, emotional, and behavioral outcomes for the students. The current state of accountability for the schools prevents schools from trying out new methods, and they are restricted to activities that were a part of the core curriculum alone (Antinluoma et al., 2021). Nearly three years ago, the ELLN intervention program in line with the K- to 12 Curriculum came into the story, which implements age-appropriate teaching approaches drawn from the following: Johaan Heinrich Pestalozzi's theory that children learn through a sense of observation and perception, John Locke's emphasis on learning through play, Jean Piaget's research that children learn through stages of development, Lev Vygotsky Albert Bandura and Erik Erikson's theory of socio-emotional development, and Maria Montessori and Friedrich Froebel's curriculum from real life practices (Roopnarine et al., 2015). Studies indicate that teachers who are professionally developed are better poised to support students' academic achievement (Neumann & Hood, 2009) and have a cumulative impact on higher grades, depending on environmental settings (Dodge, et al., 2022). Moreover, a child's reading readiness begins soon after birth, depending on the child's health conditions. The oral speech patterns that a child hears in his/her environment provide the necessary groundwork for learning how to read. Human language acquisition develops naturally (Anderson, & Ben Jaafar, 2003) while reading does not; learning how to read is a taught process, and reading is the foundation of academic success. One characteristic of children who begin the primary grades with difficulty reading is a lack of prior earned knowledge and skills in alphabet recognition and phonics or basic reading and writing abilities (Such, 2021). The students who struggle with reading and writing in the primary grades could be the product of a lack of reading readiness, health problems, or impoverished backgrounds (Merga, 2020). Various preschools that provide excellent curricula, rich in reading and writing opportunities, initiate a change to decrease the number of children at risk for reading literacy difficulty; playtime in pleasant settings motivates language skills, cognitive development, social skills, and preschool writing skills (Quinn et al., 2022). Oral language is related to both speaking and listening components. It is a crucial part of developing the skills for written language, which include reading and writing. Normally, individuals find no need to consider the development of language as adults are already competent speakers. Thus, they do not consider what language is and how oral and written language is developed. As young children embark in their school journey, it is significant to understand areas that impact their literacy development (Anderson, 2020). In 2012 , the New curriculum program (K- to 12) initiative gave emphasis to the importance of early intervention and school readiness efforts to help children achieve individual success and accomplish societal goals toward building a better workforce (Winter & Kelley, 2008). The increase in the literature for school readiness strengthened federal commitment to early education. The preschool/ kindergarten level is then perceived to be just as important as all the other grade levels. There is still a critical need to learn more about early learning environments. The stress on the value of preschool/kindergarten education involves achieving the objectives at this age. It also highlights the negative consequences involved if children will enter grade school without earlier experience in preschool/ kindergarten education, especially in literacy development (Yoshikawa et al., 2016). In response, there is a focus on the cognitive and socialization aspects of kindergarten programs in order to help children and parents achieve successful preschool/kindergarten experiences. According Seabra-Santos et al. (2022), during the preschool years of children, teachers and parents are faced with the significant concern of evaluating if the child is ready for grade school the following year. The education process is perceived as a joint venture between the child, the family, the school, and the teachers. This is involved in the discussion of school readiness, a complex issue in education research. Barnett et al. (2020) mentioned that there is an increase in the focus on readiness in the context of early childhood education in the country because of the growing concern for failing students and schools, as determined by the NCLB assessments. The National Education Goals Panel promoted an approach for school readiness that covered five areas of child development and learning. These are physical health and motor development, socio-emotional development, approaches toward learning, literacy, cognition, and general knowledge development (Izumi-Taylor et al., 20023). The National Association of State Boards of Education points out that developing school readiness was about building the ability for children to be ready to benefit from school and readiness to learn more than the alphabet and numbers (Brown et al., 2021). It needs to be recognized that it is not appropriate to expect that children will have a common set of skills when they enter school because they come from different backgrounds. Moreover, the focus on readiness does not necessarily involve the children alone. It is also about scrutinizing the environment the children are exposed to in order to guarantee student success (Karim, 2023).Weigel and Martin (2006) noted that the development of intervention programs to help improve early literacy and school readiness skills for young children needs to be developed to address the needs of children with the help of parents, child care programs, and the community at large (Joo et al., 2020). Through this focus, educators and early childhood providers will be able to target local programs at an optimum level. Performance rating promotes better employee – employer relationship by making the employee know what his employer expects of him and how he performed his tasks terms of job requirements. It also encourages the employees to put forth their best efforts in their works toward the attainment of organizational goals. The performance appraisal points out the relative strengths and weaknesses of the people in the organization as well as the effectiveness of the system procedures used by the workers in their job. It further reveals or identifies the specific training needs of an agent.

Methodology

Research Design and Sampling Techniques: This study utilized Descriptive Quantitative Research Design. It sought to determine the issues and concerns of the different group of teachers in teaching literacy. The target respondents in this study were the Day Care Teachers, Kindergarten Teachers and Grade 1 Teachers in Sulu Province. Purposive Sampling Method was employed to gather the fifteen (15) respondents wherein, five (5) were Day Care Teachers, five (5) were kindergarten teachers and five (5) were Grade 1 teachers.

Research Instrument: To gather the professional profile of the teachers, a Demographic Profile Questionnaire was employed. To gather data on the issues of teachers, a prepared 5-point Likert scale checklist was utilized. The checklist was subdivided into three components, *the teaching strategies and readiness, pupils' readiness, and instructional support*. The checklist was consisted of twenty-two (22) items. Meanwhile, to determine the pupils' readiness, scores shall be anchored and aligned on the standardized assessment result conducted and gathered in some schools. The research instrument was subjected for validation by three experts in the field of education. The validators are Doctor of Education Degree holders and have engaged in the similar research at least in the past three years.

Data Gathering Procedure: The researcher sought permission to the principal in the administration of the instrument. Once the request was approved, the research proponent made an appointment to the teachers concerned. The respondents were asked to sign a consent form as a testimony of their willingness to participate in the research. Each respondent was given one (1) hour to accomplish the research instrument.

Data Analysis Procedure: The corresponding score of each respondent was described with an adjectival description as shown below.

Scores	Range	Adjectival Description
5	4.50-5.00	Very Evident
4	3.50-4.49	Evident
3	2.50-3.49	Moderately Evident
2	1.50-2.49	Less Evident
1	0.50-1.49	Not Evident

To answer the problem on the issues and concerns of the teachers in teaching literacy particularly in teaching strategies and readiness, contents and instructional support, individual mean was used.

Results And Discussion

Issues and concerns of the Day Care, Kinder and Grade 1 Teachers of Sulu in teaching literacy: Table 1 shows the overall result on the issues and concerns of the Day Care, Kindergarten and Grade 1 teachers of Sulu in terms of Teaching Strategies and Readiness. The combined score of the respondents of 4.24 with the adjectival description of *very evident* reveals that respondents are challenged in terms of their teaching strategies and readiness in teaching literacy to their pupils. This means, that teaching strategies and readiness among the group of teachers is one of the issues and concerns in the successful teaching of literacy. Table 1. Issues and Concerns of day care, kindergarten and grade1 teachers of Sulu on Teaching Literacy in terms of Teaching Strategies and Readiness

A.Issues and Concerns in terms of Teaching Strategies and Readiness	Score	Description
1.Teachers lack the preparation to teach	4.5	Very Evident
2.Pupils have low level of readiness and prior knowledge	4.6	Very Evident
3.Teachers lack trainings on pedagogical approaches	3.82	Very Evident
4.Teachers are not ready to teach the concepts of literacy	4.85	Very Evident
5.Teachers have limited knowledge on approaches/ teaching strategies	3.82	Very Evident

6.Teachers are not open to new teaching techniques for teaching literacy	3.82	Very Evident
Average	**4.24**	***Very Evident***

Table 2 shows the overall result on the issues and concerns of the teacher-respondents in terms of Pupils' Readiness. The result shows that eight (8) out of thirteen (13) items are described as not evident, four (4) of the items are moderately evident and one (1) as less evident. This means that teachers found that most learners are not ready or are not equipped with prerequisite skills to learn literacy. On the other hand, teachers found that some learners are moderately ready with some competencies/areas such as in Alphabet knowledge, Communicating with peers in mother tongue, Communicating with peers in English, Understanding instructions in mother tongue and less ready on the area of Responding to simple questions when ask in mother tongue. However, when looking at the average score of the teacher-respondents, the result shows that teachers found that learners are not ready at all to learn literacy as manifested in the combined score of 1.38 with a description of Not Evident. This implies then that Pupil's Readiness is a factor that impedes successful literacy learning among the learners, hence, considered as one of the issues confronting the teachers in the teaching of literacy.

Table 2. Issues and Concerns of day care, kindergarten and grade1 teachers of Sulu on Teaching Literacy in terms of Pupils Readiness

B.Issues and Concerns in	Score	Description

Pupils' Readiness		
1.Alphabet knowledge	2.82	Moderately Evident
2.Phonemic Awareness	1.00	Not Evident
3.Phonics and word recognition	1.20	Not Evident
4.Vocabulary and comprehension	.75	Not Evident
5.Fluency (reading with automaticity and prosody)	.50	Not Evident
6.Holding pencil/ball pen properly	.25	Not Evident
7.Writing legibly in print/cursive	.55	Not Evident
8.Responding to simple questions when ask in mother tongue	2.00	Less Evident
9.Responding to simple questions when ask in English	.25	Not Evident
10.Communicating with peers in mother tongue	2.82	Moderately Evident
11.Communicating with peers in English	2.82	Moderately Evident
12.Understanding instructions in mother tongue	2.82	Moderately Evident
13.Understanding instructions in English	.20	Not Evident
Average	*1.38*	*Not Evident*

Table 3 presents the result on the issues and concerns of the teachers in terms of Instructional Support. The combined score of 4.41 with a descriptive rating of **Very Evident** tells that the teachers are challenged in terms of the support received from the school head, parents and stakeholders in the execution of their instructional activities. It implies that teachers receive minimal support thus making the instructional support as one of the issues and concerns requiring attention in order to successfully carry out literacy teaching and reading among the learners in Sulu Division. Table 3. Issues and Concerns of day care, kindergarten and grade1 teachers of Sulu on Teaching Literacy in terms of Instructional Support

Issues and Concerns in terms of Teaching Instructional Support	Score	Description
Teachers receive minimal support from the school heads on their instructional inputs	4.6	Very Evident
Parents and stakeholders show low support on the different school programs	4.82	Very Evident
There are no enough funds to support teaching activities	3.82	Very Evident
Average	4.41	Very Evident

Conclusion: The different issues and concerns of the day care, kindergarten and grade 1 teachers in teaching Literacy were found in the study, to wit; teaching strategies and readiness, pupils' readiness and instructional support. It was found that different issues under the teaching strategies and readiness were evident that affect the performance of the teachers in teaching literacy and these include Teachers lack the preparation to teach, Pupils have low level of readiness and prior knowledge, Teachers lack trainings on pedagogical approaches, Teachers are not ready to teach the concepts of literacy, Teachers have limited knowledge on approaches/ teaching strategies and Teachers are not open to new teaching techniques for teaching literacy. Meanwhile, Teachers receive minimal support from the school heads on their instructional inputs, Parents and stakeholders show low support on the different school programs and There are no enough funds to support teaching activities were among the issues found under instructional support that likewise affect the teaching literacy among the teachers. Furthermore, this study further reveals that pupils' readiness is also an issue and concern in teaching literacy. The respondents found that most of the learners are not equipped with the competencies or do not have good disposition towards the different areas such as Phonemic Awareness, Phonics and word recognition, Vocabulary and comprehension, Fluency (reading with automaticity and prosody), Holding pencil/ball pen properly, Writing legibly in print/cursive, Responding to simple questions when ask in English and Understanding instructions in English. Although in some areas as in Alphabet knowledge, Communicating with peers in mother tongue, Communicating with peers in English, Understanding instructions in mother tongue and Responding to simple questions when ask in mother tongue, learners are found to be less and moderately ready. This implies further that learners are not equipped enough with all the competencies for reading that will make them ready for admission to the higher level since these are foundational skills for learning. Teachers issues and concerns on having rigid training on the skills to teach literacy are but their common apprehension for the lack of strategies to teach. Hence, majority of those respondents gave the same clamor to attend a training to advance their knowledge in teaching.

Recommendations

The school administration may sponsor seminars and intensive supplemental trainings to teach reading and to update the day care, kindergarten and grade1 teachers with the result of this study. Teachers shall undergo assessment of skills in reading likewise be tested on all competencies requisite to reading. Post training assessment shall also be done to measure the extent of the progress after attending the training. Extended Monitoring and evaluation shall be done quarterly to monitor cascading and usage of concepts. Teachers may conceive activities/programs that may strengthen parents and stakeholders support towards literacy activities in school. School heads may extend and resources to support the conduct of literacy activities in classrooms. Future researchers may work on the same study by considering a wider scope on variables and population to further validate the findings of this study.

References

1. Anderson, A. L. (2020). Anne's Transatlantic Imagination: Reading as Travel in Anne of Green Gables. In *Reading Transatlantic Girlhood in the Long Nineteenth Century* (pp. 58-76). Routledge.

2. Anderson, S. E., & Ben Jaafar, S. (2003). Policy trends in Ontario education. *ICEC Working, Anais... Toronto, set.*

3. Ansari, A., Pianta, R. C., Whittaker, J. E., Vitiello, V., & Ruzek, E. (2021). Enrollment in public-prekindergarten and school readiness skills at kindergarten entry: Differential associations by home language, income, and program characteristics. *Early Childhood Research Quarterly*, *54*, 60-71.

4. Antinluoma, M., Ilomäki, L., & Toom, A. (2021, April). Practices of professional learning communities. In *Frontiers in education* (Vol. 6, p. 617613). Frontiers Media SA.

5. Barnett, M. A., Paschall, K. W., Mastergeorge, A. M., Cutshaw, C. A., & Warren, S. M. (2020). Influences of parent engagement in early childhood education centers and the home on kindergarten school readiness. *Early Childhood Research Quarterly*, *53*, 260-273.

6. Barratt-Pugh, C., & Rohl, M. (Eds.). (2020). *Literacy learning in the early years*. Routledge.

7. Birgisdottir, F., Gestsdottir, S., & Geldhof, G. J. (2020). Early predictors of first and fourth grade reading and math: The role of self-regulation and early literacy skills. *Early Childhood Research Quarterly*, *53*, 507-519.

8. Brown, C. P., Barry, D. P., & Ku, D. H. (2021). How education stakeholders made sense of school readiness in and beyond kindergarten. *Journal of Research in Childhood Education*, *35*(1), 122-142.

9. DepEd. (2012). DepEd Order No. 31, series 2012. Policy Guidelines on the Implementation of Grades 1 to 10 of the K

to 12 Basic Education Curriculum (BEC) Effective School Year 2012-2013.

10. Dodge, D. T., Colker, L. J., & Heroman, C. (2002). *Connecting content, teaching, and learning: The creative curriculum for preschool.* Teaching Strategies, Inc., PO Box 42243, Washington, DC 20015.

11. Durlak, J. A., Mahoney, J. L., & Boyle, A. E. (2022). What we know, and what we need to find out about universal, school-based social and emotional learning programs for children and adolescents: A review of meta-analyses and directions for future research. *Psychological Bulletin, 148*(11-12), 765.

12. Hampel, R. (2008). Progressive versus traditional education. Retrieved August 11, 2010, from http://www.faqs.org/childhood/Pa-Re/Progressive-Education.html

13. Izumi-Taylor, S., Li, Y., & Ro, Y. (2023). Promoting preschoolers' gross motor developmen through literature and movement activities. *The Dragon Lode, 41*(2), 16-20.

14. Joo, Y. S., Magnuson, K., Duncan, G. J., Schindler, H. S., Yoshikawa, H., & Ziol-Guest, K. M. (2020). What works in early childhood education programs?: A meta–analysis of preschool enhancement programs. *Early Education and Development, 31*(1), 1-26.

15. Karim, S. (2023). Inclusive Education for Students With Diverse Learning Needs in Mainstream Schools.

In *Interdisciplinary Perspectives on Special and Inclusive Education in a Volatile, Uncertain, Complex & Ambiguous (Vuca) World* (pp. 137-156). Emerald Publishing Limited.

16. Kilag, O. K. T., Ignacio, R., Lumando, E. B., Alvez, G. U., Abendan, C. F. K., QuiÃƒÂ±anola, N. A. M. P., & Sasan, J. M. (2022). ICT Integration in Primary School Classrooms in the time of Pandemic in the Light of Jean Piaget's Cognitive Development Theory. *International Journal of Emerging Issues in Early Childhood Education*, 4(2), 42-54.

17. Lehrl, S., Rossbach, H. G., & Weinert, S. (2024). Fostering Early Competence Development Through Home and Preschool Learning Environments—a Summary of Findings from the BiKS-3-18 Study. In *Educational Processes, Decisions, and the Development of Competencies from Early Preschool Age to Adolescence: Findings from the BiKS Cohort Panel Studies* (pp. 163-190). Wiesbaden: Springer Fachmedien Wiesbaden.

18. Looi, C. K., Wong, S. L., Kong, S. C., Chan, T. W., Shih, J. L., Chang, B., ... & Liao, C. C. (2023). Interest-Driven Creator Theory: case study of embodiment in an experimental school in Taiwan. *Research and Practice in Technology Enhanced Learning*, *18*, 023-023.

19. Mann, J., Gray, T., Truong, S., Brymer, E., Passy, R., Ho, S., ... & Cowper, R. (2022). Getting out of the classroom and into nature: a systematic review of nature-specific outdoor learning

on school Children's learning and development. *Frontiers in Public Health*, *10*, 877058.

20.Merga, M. K. (2020). "Fallen through the cracks": Teachers' perceptions of barriers faced by struggling literacy learners in secondary school. *English in Education*, *54*(4), 371-395.

21.Mirzajonova, E. T., & Parpiyeva, O. R. (2022). Modern special preschool education: problems and solutions. *Journal of Pedagogical Inventions and Practices*, *9*, 100-106.

22.Morales, M. P. E., Abulon, E. L. R., Soriano, P. R., David, A. P., Hermosisima, M. V. C., & Gerundio, M. G. (2016). Examining teachers' conception of and needs on action research. *Issues in Educational Research*, *26*(3), 464-489.

23.Mullis, I. V. S., Martin, M. O., Foy, P., Kelly, D. L., & Fishbein, B. (2020). TIMSS 2019 international results in mathematics and science. https://timssandpirls.bc.edu/timss2019/international-results

24.Neumann, D. L., & Hood, M. (2009). The effects of using a wiki on student engagement and learning of report writing skills in a university statistics course. *Australasian journal of educational technology*, *25*(3).

25.Phiri, M., Thelma, C. C., & Mwanapabu, N. H. (2024). The Effect of Using Local Languages as A Medium of Instruction on Academic Performance of Learners: A Case of Selected Primary Schools in Solwezi District of North-Western

Province, Zambia. *International Journal of Novel Research in Humanity and Social Sciences, 11*(3), 9-26.

26. Quinn, M. F., Gerde, H. K., & Bingham, G. E. (2022). Who, what, and where: Classroom contexts for preschool writing experiences. *Early Education and Development, 33*(8), 1439-1460.

27. Roopnarine, J., Patte, M., Johnson, J., & Kuschner, D. (2015). *International perspectives on children's play*. McGraw-Hill Education (UK).

28. Seabra-Santos, M., Major, S., Patras, J., Pereira, M., Pimentel, M., Baptista, E., ... & Gaspar, M. F. (2022). Transition to primary school of children in economic disadvantage: Does a preschool teacher training program make a difference?. *Early Childhood Education Journal, 50*(6), 1071-1081.

29. Such, C. (2021). The art and science of teaching primary reading. *The Art and Science of Teaching Primary Reading*, 1-100.

30. Vaisarova, J., & Reynolds, A. J. (2022). Is more child-initiated always better? Exploring relations between child-initiated instruction and preschoolers' school readiness. *Educational assessment, evaluation and accountability, 34*(2), 195-226.

31. Wang, B., Luo, X., Yue, A., Tang, L., & Shi, Y. (2022). Family environment in rural China and the link with early childhood development. *Early child development and care, 192*(4), 617-630.

32. Wilcox, M. J., Gray, S., & Reiser, M. (2020). Preschoolers with developmental speech and/or language impairment: Efficacy of

the Teaching Early Literacy and Language (TELL) curriculum. *Early Childhood Research Quarterly*, *51*, 124-143.

33. Winter, S. M., & Kelley, M. F. (2008). Forty years of school readiness research: What have we learned?. *Childhood Education*, *84*(5), 260-266.

34. Yidirim, B. (2021). Preschool STEM activities: Preschool teachers' preparation and views. *Early Childhood Education Journal*, *49*(2), 149-162.

35. Yoshikawa, H., Weiland, C., & Brooks-Gunn, J. (2016). When does preschool matter?. *The Future of Children*, 21-35.

2. Analysis of Animal Derivatives and Lead in Unregistered Eye Makeup Products.

Ambray, Shannen Tiffany C., de Real, Yala Hope P., Diaz, Ira Grant N., Panaguiton, Emerald Sheen I., Radzak, Walid S., Reyes, Cesar Armand F., Sablay, Eunice S and Faller, Erwin M.

Pharmacy Department, San Pedro College; shambray04@gmail.com
12 Guzman St, Poblacion District, Davao City, Davao del Sur, **Philippines**

Abstract: The presence of haram-contaminated products has been a longstanding concern for global Muslim communities, with cosmetics emerging as a particularly under-regulated sector compared to food and personal care items. This regulatory gap poses a significant safety risk to both Muslim and non-Muslim consumers due to the well-known inclusion of animal derivatives and lead in cosmetics, which can be absorbed through skin contact. Extensive exposure, even to minimal lead levels, has been associated with specific cancers and health risks. Unregistered makeup brands, lacking government authentication and necessary halal certifications, are particularly implicated in this issue. To address this concern, this study specifically examines the presence of haram components—lead and animal derivatives from porcine, bovine, and equine sources—in unregistered eye makeup products. Nine (9) diverse samples from various brands in Davao City underwent quantitative testing using atomic absorption spectroscopy (AAS) for lead, and real-time polymerase chain reaction (RT-PCR) for animal derivatives. All samples were found free of forbidden animal-derived ingredients, contradicting initial expectations. However, two makeup brands tested positive for lead contamination. In conclusion, this study asserts that, with the exception of certain eyeshadow brands, eye makeup products in Davao City generally conform to halal requirements. The data at hand suggest that unregistered eye mascara, eye liner, are generally considered safe for consumer use as a cheap and local alternative for known cosmetic brands. However, the lack of certification of registration from the Food and Drug Administration (FDA) still emphasizes the need for increased scrutiny of unregistered cosmetic brands and reinforced regulatory measures to ensure consumer safety.

Keywords: haram components, animal-derived ingredients, lead, unregistered makeup products, Food and Drug Administration (FDA)

Introduction: The halal authentication of many consumer goods pose a significant concern for Muslims due to the possible presence of haram ingredients, which extends beyond food to personal care products, particularly, cosmetic products. Cosmetic products widely available around the globe are manufactured by non-Muslim producers whose processes may not meet the necessary standards of halal science (Sugibayashi *et al.*, 2019). Accordingly, most of today's makeup products cater to non-Muslim consumers without assurance of the ingredients' acceptability within the Islamic community. According to the followers of the Islamic faith, the consumption or the use of haram, which directly translates to unlawful or impermissible, is prohibited as it is detrimental to their physical health, moral character, and most importantly, their religion (Hassan, Ahmad, & Zain, 2018). Various manufacturers still incorporate animal derivatives in cosmetics, such as collagen, a popular ingredient in many of today's makeup (Cristiano, Guagni, 2022). For these ingredients to be classified as halal, their animal sources must be slaughtered in accordance with Islamic Law (Alexander, 2021). As such, Muslims face difficulty in verifying cosmetic ingredients' acceptability. Hence, there are still several challenges in the development of halal cosmetics (Sugibayashi *et al.*, 2019). In the Philippines, efforts have been made to regulate halal cosmetics due to the growing demand of halal certified products. The Bureau of Philippine Standards (DTI-BPS) issued a Philippine National Standard (PNS) for halal cosmetics to aid local manufacturers (DTI, 2022). Using plant derivatives and other synthetic ingredients in the manufacture of halal cosmetics would lessen the doubt about the product's halal authentication. It would appeal more to the consumers (Sugibayashi *et al.*, 2019). Aside from the presence of haram components, the proliferation of unregistered beauty products affects not only Muslims but non-halal consumers as well, as it may pose a significant risk to the safety of the users. FDA warned that the potential hazard might come from the ingredients that must not be used in cosmetics or from the contamination of heavy metals like mercury in many cosmetic products (Crisostomo, 2017). There is widespread availability of unregistered eye cosmetics in Davao City, which do not have any halal certification to verify that it is free of haram ingredients. There is limited literature to address this problem, especially at the local level. To address this gap, the study aims to identify the components present and determine the halal authentication of unregistered eye makeup products within Davao City. **Methods: Study Design:** This study employs a quantitative experimental research design using a descriptive method, wherein the different unregistered eye makeup products in Davao City gathered by the researchers will undergo tests to determine the haram components, namely animal derivatives and heavy metals present in each product, as well heavy metals contents in unregistered eye makeup products, and to discern whether unregistered eye makeup products used for this study are halal. **Data Analysis:** In order to determine if the unregistered eye makeup products in Davao City are classified as haram/halal, RT-PCR is used to detect the presence of animal derivatives (Erwanto, 2018). Similarly, AAS is used to detect the presence of lead in unregistered eye makeup products (Prabhas et al., 2018). There will be three (3) different eye makeup products, namely, eye shadow, mascara, eye liner, each with three (3) different brands. A total of nine (9) samples shall be utilized for each test. The data gathered from the study is analyzed and interpreted using the following statistical tests:.**One-way ANOVA test.** A one-way ANOVA test determines whether a significant difference exists between three or more groups (JMP, 2020). In this study, a one-way ANOVA shall be used to determine if there is a significant difference in the presence of haram components between the eye makeup, namely, eye shadow, eyeliner, and mascara.

Results And Discussion

Upon performing a series of analytical tests to detect the presence of metal and animal contaminants, the results indicate a minimal to considerable risk in using unregistered eye makeup products. The nine (9) samples of unregistered cosmetics collected within the scope of Davao City have been thoroughly assessed to identify the presence of lead and animal derivatives.

Table 1. Summary of Lead Content

Sample	Lead	Exposure	Implication
Mascara A	0 ppm	Null	Safe
Mascara B	0 ppm	Null	Safe
Mascara C	0 ppm	Null	Safe
Eye Liner A	0 ppm	Null	Safe
Eye Liner B	0 ppm	Null	Safe
Eye Liner C	0 ppm	Null	Safe
Eye Shadow A	0 ppm	Null	Safe
Eye Shadow B	247 ppm	High	High risk
Eye Shadow C	9.2 ppm	Low	Safe but with minimal risk

Permissible Limit: *NMT 20 mg/kg or 20 mg/L (20 ppm) when tested by ASEAN Cosmetic Method* The lead analysis using AAS revealed 2 out of 9 samples that tested positive for containing lead. Specifically, the results show that eye shadow brand B contains 247 ppm, which exceeds the permissible limit of lead formed in cosmetics. On the other hand, Eye Shadow Brand C is within the acceptable limit and is considered safe for consumer use. According to the ASEAN Guidelines on Limits of Contaminants for Cosmetics (2017), heavy metal impurities like lead should not be more than 20 mg/kg or 20 mg/L (20 ppm) when tested by the ASEAN Cosmetic Method. ASEAN has established these guidelines to ensure that any presence of contaminants in cosmetics is kept within the allowable limit and that lead impurities exceeding the permissible range are unsafe and, therefore, unfit for consumer use. A similar result was obtained by Agra, Daileg et al. (2019), where Chemical Analysis of Heavy Metals in Organic, Counterfeit, and Local Brand Lipsticks is carried out using a Hydride Vapor Generation Technique – AAS. The results show traces of heavy metals on four samples within the permissible limit. The lipstick containing natural ingredients has the most negligible concentration of heavy metal impurities. However, the general safety of counterfeit lipstick is not guaranteed since one sample contains an alarming amount of heavy metal impurities, and the highest systemic exposure dose can be obtained from lead in counterfeit lipstick.

Table 2. Summary of Animal Derivatives

Brand	Porcine DNA	Bovine DNA	Equine

			DNA
Mascara A	0 ppm	0 ppm	0 ppm
Mascara B	0 ppm	0 ppm	0 ppm
Mascara C	0 ppm	0 ppm	0 ppm
Eye Liner A	0 ppm	0 ppm	0 ppm
Eye Liner B	0 ppm	0 ppm	0 ppm
Eye Liner C	0 ppm	0 ppm	0 ppm
Eye Shadow A	0 ppm	0 ppm	0 ppm
Eye Shadow B	0 ppm	0 ppm	0 ppm
Eye Shadow C	0 ppm	0 ppm	0 ppm

The cosmetic products gathered were screened for the following: porcine DNA, bovine DNA, and equine DNA. Results showcased a negative result across all of the cosmetic brands tested, which means that based on this criteria alone, unregistered eye makeup is halal, and is permissible for use of Muslims. The evidence supporting the results can be reinforced through the Halal Cosmetics Expo (2020), which states that halal cosmetics refer to beauty products that have been manufactured and composed of ingredients permissible under Islamic Shariah (law). In addition, the work of Iman Balagam (2023) points out that the term 'halal-certified' is most often used to refer to a product that does not contain alcohol, pork, or animal-derived ingredients that do not comply with Islamic rituals. Table 3.1 One-Way Anova of Lead in Eye Makeup

Source of Variation	SS	df	MS	F	P-value	Decision
Between Groups	14586.32	2	7293.16	1.115897	0.387231	Accept null hypothesis
Within Groups	39214.16	6	6535.693			

Total	53800.48	8				

Correlation at the level of 0.05 (Two-tailed)

The ANOVA test was conducted to determine if there is a significant difference between the different brands of eye makeup in terms of lead content. The p-value for each group comparison is greater than 0.5, while the alpha level for the ANOVA test is 0.05, which indicates that the probability of making a Type I error (concluding that there is a significant difference when there is not) is 5%. The decision column shows the decision of the hypothesis test. In this case, the null hypothesis is that there is no significant difference in the presence of lead among the three (3) types of eye makeup products: mascara, eye liner, and eye shadow. Since the p-value for each group comparison is greater than 0.05, we fail to reject the null hypothesis. This means that there is not enough evidence to conclude that there is a statistically significant difference between the lead content of the three groups.

Table 3.2 One-Way Anova of Animal Derivatives in Eye Makeup

Source of Variation	SS	df	MS	F	P-value	Decision
Between Groups	0	2	0			Accept null hypothe sis
Within Groups	0	6	0	65535	0	
Total	0	8				

Correlation at the level of 0.05 (Two-tailed) The absence of animal derivatives in all samples yields a p-value of 0, greater than 0.05, therefore, fails to reject the null hypothesis. This indicates that there is no significant difference in the animal derivatives between the nine (9) makeup samples.

Conclusion: The main objective of this study was to identify the presence of haram components in unregistered eye makeup, specifically lead and animal derivatives of porcine, bovine, and equine sources. With the analyses conducted and the findings drawn, it can be concluded that there is no significant difference in the haram components in the samples. Of the three categories of eye makeup chosen for this study, mascara, eyeliner, and eye shadow, selected brands under eye shadow are haram due to high lead levels. AAS was employed for all nine (9) samples, divided into the three classifications of eye makeup used in this study to determine the presence and quantity of lead accurately. The test revealed that only brand B and brand C under eye shadow contain traces of lead, with brand B exceeding the allowable limit when tested by the ASEAN Cosmetic Method. As for the animal-derived ingredients, the study has chosen porcine, bovine, and equine animal sources as the components to be tested. Using RT-PCR, results have revealed that the nine (9) samples across all brands contain no prohibited animal-derived ingredients. With these results, the researchers conclude that only unregistered mascara and eyeliner products found within Davao City are acceptable for Muslim consumers. The absence of lead and animal derivatives signifies that the ingredients found in the cosmetics are halal, which contributes to the overall safety and acceptability of unregistered cosmetic products. Overall, the study emphasizes that unregistered eye makeup within Davao City is halal-compliant and acceptable for the Muslim Community, except for eye shadows. Careful consideration and care must be taken upon choosing unregistered eye shadow due to the possible risk of lead contamination.

References

1. Alexander, A. (2021, April 20). Everything You Need to Know About the Halal Cosmetic Industry. Retrieved September 22, 2022, from https://www.halalwatchworld.org/everything-you-need-to-know-about-the-halal-cosmetic-industry

2. Association of South East Asian Nations (ASEAN). (2017, May 3). ASEAN Guidelines on Limits of Contaminants for Cosmetics. ASEAN. https://www.hsa.gov.sg/docs/default-source/hprg-cosmetics/asean-guidelines-on-limits-of-contaminants-for-cosmetics-ver-3.pdf

3. Balagam, I. (2023, February 3). What makes a beauty product halal? There's more to it than you think. Byrdie. https://www.byrdie.com/how-to-tell-if-makeup-is-halal-7098402

4. Cristiano, L. (2022, January 19). Zooceuticals and Cosmetic Ingredients Derived from Animals. Retrieved September 26, 2022, from https://www.mdpi.com/2079-9284/9/1/13/htm

5. Daileg, J. A., De Ocampo, C. J., Domingo, C. D., Guerrero, M. I., Torres, K. G., & Agra, A. J. (2019, August 2). Chemical analysis of heavy metals in organic, counterfeit and local brand lipsticks using hydride vapor generation technique –atomic absorption spectroscopy. Edu.Ph. Retrieved August 20, 2023, from https://lpulaguna.edu.ph/wp-content/uploads/2019/10/2.-Chemical-Analysis-of-Heavy-Metals-in-Organic-Counterfeit-And-Local-Brand-Lipsticks-Using-Hydride-Vapor-Generation-Technique-%E2%80%93Atomic-Absorption-Spectroscopy.pdf

6. DTI. (2022, March 25). DTI-BPS promulgates standard on Halal cosmetics. Retrieved September 24, 2022, from https://www.dti.gov.ph/archives/news-archives/dti-bps-promulgates-standard-on-halal-cosmetics/

7. Erwanto, Y. (2018). Molecular based method using PCR technology on porcine derivative detection for halal authentication. In I. Abdurakhmonov (Ed.), Genotyping. InTech.

8. FDA. (2022, March 3). FDA's Testing of Cosmetics for Arsenic, Cadmium, Chromium, Cobalt, Lead, Mercury, and Nickel Content. Retrieved October 31, 2022, from https://www.fda.gov/cosmetics/potential-contaminants-

cosmetics/fdas-testing-cosmetics-arsenic-cadmium-chromium-cobalt-lead-mercury-and-nickel-content#surveyed_metals

9. Halal Cosmetics Expo. (2020, September 17). *Halal certification & the halal industry*. In-Cosmetics Connect | The in-Cosmetics Group Is the Meeting Point and Learning Hub for the Personal Care Development Community Worldwide; in-cosmetics Connect. https://connect.in-cosmetics.com/regions/halal-cosmetics/halal-certification-and-the-halal-cosmetics-industry/

10. Hassan, N., Ahmad, T., & Zain, N. M. (2018, November 15). Chemical and Chemometric Methods for Halal Authentication of Gelatin: An Overview. Retrieved September 25, 2022, from https://ift.onlinelibrary.wiley.com/doi/10.1111/1750-3841.14370

11. One-way ANOVA. (2020, July 20). Jmp.com. Retrieved September 27, 2022, from https://www.jmp.com/en_ph/statistics-knowledge-portal/one-way-anova.html

12. Sugibayashi, K. (2019, July 1). Halal Cosmetics: A Review on Ingredients, Production, and Testing Methods. Retrieved September 22, 2022, from https://www.mdpi.com/2079-9284/6/3/37/htm

3. The Impact of Digital Banking on Customer Experience and Loyalty in Liberia's Banking Industry.

Joseph N. Wonnah[1] and Charles F. Johnson[2]

[1]Master of International Business, Beijing Technology and Business University, **China**

[2]Master of Economic Development, Renmin University of China, **China**

Abstract: The banking sector in Liberia has undergone a significant digital transformation, with Guaranty Trust Bank Liberia Limited (GT Bank Liberia) at the forefront of this revolution. This study investigates the impact of digital banking on customer satisfaction and loyalty within the Liberian context. A survey-based quantitative research design was employed, targeting a sample of 915 customers from GT Bank in Liberia. The findings revealed a positive and significant impact of digital banking on customer loyalty. Specifically, the regression analysis demonstrated that a 1% increase in digital banking usage is associated with 33% customer loyalty (p=0.000) and 62% increase in customer satisfaction quality (p=0.002). The descriptive statistics further corroborated these findings, with 80% of respondents acknowledging that available digital banking enhances their loyalty to the bank. However, areas for improvement were identified, such as minimizing website downtime (positive skewness) and enhancing record-keeping accuracy (79% agreed). The study contributes to the understanding of the transformative role of digital banking in the Liberian banking sector, providing comprehensive understanding to GT Bank Liberia and other financial institutions to strengthen their digital banking capabilities, foster deeper customer engagement, and enhance long-term customer loyalty. Recommendations include enhancing digital infrastructure, implementing personalized experiences, embracing omnichannel integration, and exploring emerging technologies.

Keywords: Digital banking, customer satisfaction, customer loyalty, Liberian banking sector, GT Bank Liberia

Introduction: Digital marketing involves promoting and advertising products, services, and brands through various digital channels and technologies. This includes strategies such as search engine optimization (SEO), social media marketing, email marketing, content marketing, and online advertising. The main goal of digital marketing is to connect with and engage a specific audience via platforms like websites, social media, search engines, and mobile apps (Antonio et al., 2022). Through digital marketing, businesses can establish personalized and interactive connections with customers, monitor and analyze campaign performance, and adjust strategies as needed (Qian et al., 2023). In Liberia, the banking sector has seen significant growth and transformation in recent years, largely due to the integration of digital banking services. This shift towards digital solutions has been a key driver of the banking industry's growth and competitive edge. Guaranty Trust Bank Liberia Limited (GT Bank Liberia), a subsidiary of the Nigerian-based Guaranty Trust Bank PLC, has been at the forefront of this digital revolution in the Liberian banking landscape. Guaranty Trust Bank was established in Liberia on June 7, 2007, and officially licensed for operation on March 6, 2009. The bank offers a diverse range of services, including institutional investment, commercial and retail banking, financial advisory, and capital financing for small to medium and medium long-term needs (GT Bank Liberia Limited). As a subsidiary of Nigeria's Guaranty Trust Bank PLC, which boasts a Triple rating, GT Bank Liberia benefits from the strong backing of its reputable parent company. Notably, it was the first new-generation indigenous African bank to obtain a banking license for full-fledged operations in the United Kingdom.Currently, GTBank PLC, Nigeria, holds a substantial 99.43% of the issued share capital of the Liberian bank, with the remaining 0.57% held by esteemed Liberian individuals. This ownership structure underscores the bank's authority and influence in the market. GT Bank Liberia operates from eight strategic business locations across the country: Clara Town, Randall Street, Redlight, Sinkor, Waterside, RIA, Ganta, and Buchanan. Despite the significant progress in the Liberian banking sector, there is a crucial need to understand the impact of digital banking initiatives on customer relations. Specifically, questions remain about the effectiveness of digital banking at GT Bank Liberia in enhancing customer service quality and its effects on customer loyalty in an increasingly competitive banking landscape. This study aims to address these concerns.

The objective of the Study: The study examines the effectiveness of digital banking at GT Bank Liberia in enhancing customer satisfaction quality and its effects on customer loyalty. Specifically, it:

i. Assesses the impact of digital banking on customer satisfaction quality at GT Bank Liberia Limited; and

ii. Evaluates the effects of digital banking on customer loyalty.

Research Questions: The research questions that guide the study are as follows:

i. What are the effects of Digital banking on Customer Loyalty?

ii. How does Digital Banking at GT Bank Liberia influence overall Customer Satisfaction Quality?

Research Methodology: The study utilized a survey design to gather necessary data, focusing on digital banking as a factor influencing customer satisfaction quality and customer loyalty at GT Bank Liberia-Limited. The survey method, deemed suitable for the research goal, aligns with previous studies (Uwalaka & Eze, 2020; Idowu & Fadiman, 2015). The research population comprised customers from GTBank, chosen through purposive sampling based on criteria such as using a digital banking platform for the past year and being 18 years or older. The research adopted Umbas' regression model (2017) to assess the stimulating effect of digital banking on customer satisfaction quality and customer loyalty. As such, the functional model for the study is expressed as:

$$CSQ = f(DB) ----------------(1)$$

Where: CSQ represents Customer Satisfaction and DB stands for Digital Banking. Generally, the study has two main objectives:

1) To assess the effect of digital banking on customer service quality, thus, we expressed the econometric model as:

$$CSQ = \beta 0 + \beta 1DB + \mu ----------(2)$$

2) To evaluate the effects of digital banking on customer loyalty at GT Bank in Liberia, represented by the econometric model:

$$CL = \beta 0 + \beta 1DB + \mu -----------(3)$$

In these models, *CSQ* stands for customer service quality, *DB* represents digital banking, *CL* for customer loyalty, *β0* for regression constant, and *β1* for regression coefficients of digital banking.

Sample Size and Data Source: Sample sizes was determined using Taro Yamane's formula, resulting in a total sample size of 915 customers. Thereafter, a self-administered questionnaire was developed for data collection. The questions were derived from the study objectives. **Data Analysis & Robustness Check:** The collected data were analyzed using descriptive statistics, including mean scores and standard deviation. Additionally, regression analysis was employed to examine relationships among the variables. Furthermore, the researchers assessed the reliability of the measurement scales employed in the study by calculating Cronbach's alpha. A value above 0.7 for this statistic suggested satisfactory internal consistency among the scale items. To bolster the credibility of their results, the investigators performed a series of diagnostic checks. These included tests for multicollinearity (excessive correlation among predictor variables), heteroscedasticity (non-constant variance of errors), and normality of residuals (deviations from the fitted model following a normal distribution).

Results

Descriptive Statistics: This section presents the findings and discussion of the data analysis in the study. *Table 1 displays the* descriptive statistics of the obtained responses.

Table 1: Descriptive Statistics of Obtained Responses

Statistic	CSQ	CL	DBAP
N (Valid)	915	915	915
Missing	0	0	0
Mean	4.180	4.184	6.164
Std. Deviation	0.08893	0.0888	0.1408
Minimum	3.0	3.0	3.0
Maximum	6.0	6.0	7.0

Note: CSQ = Customer Satisfaction Quality, CL = Customer Loyalty, DB = Digital Banking

In this study, there are 915 valid observations for all three variables, with no missing data. The mean values for Customer Satisfaction Quality, Customer Loyalty, and Digital Banking are 4.180, 4.184, and

6.164, respectively. The standard deviations are 0.08893 for Customer Satisfaction Quality, 0.0888 for Customer Loyalty, and 0.1408 for Digital Banking. The minimum value for all three variables is 3.0. The maximum values are 6.0 for both Customer Satisfaction Quality and Customer Loyalty, and 7.0 for Digital Banking. **The Effect of Digital Banking on Customer Loyalty:** *Table 3: The Effective of Digital Banking on Customer Loyalty*

Dependent Variable: Customer Loyalty	Statistics
DB	0.339
Std. Error	0.031
Beta	10.800
t-statistics	9.117
F-statistics	72.520
Sig.	0.000
Adjusted R^2	0.483
Durbin-Watson Statistics	2.094

The study investigated the relationship between digital banking and customer satisfaction quality at GT Bank Liberia Limited. The analysis included digital banking (DB) as the independent variable. The results showed a positive coefficient of 0.339 for customer loyalty, indicating a significant positive relationship between digital banking and customer loyalty. This implies that a 1% increase in digital banking adoption corresponded to a 33% increase in customer loyalty. The beta value of 0.339 also suggested a moderate effect size of customer loyalty on customer satisfaction quality. The t-statistic of 9.117, F-statistic of

72.520 with a p-value of 0.000, and an adjusted R-squared of 0.483 demonstrated the robustness and significance of the overall estimate. The Durbin-Watson statistic of 2.894 indicated no significant autocorrelation in the residuals. The descriptive statistics supported the inferential analysis. During the survey, 80% of customers agreed that digital banking reduces errors, with a mean score of 4.84 and a low error risk of 0.616. All respondents (80%) reported successful transactions on the first attempt, highlighting perceived reliability. Website downtime was minimal, with a positive skewness. Regarding record accuracy, 79% agreed, contributing to digital banking loyalty and a positively skewed distribution. All respondents acknowledged that available digital banking enhances their loyalty to the bank. When asked if their loyalty could be enhanced with available digital banking, all respondents agreed that accessible digital banking services would increase their loyalty to the bank. **Digital Banking (DB) on Customer Satisfaction Quality:** *Table 2: The Effect of Digital Banking on Customer Satisfaction Quality*

Dependent Variable: Customer Satisfaction Quality	Statistics
DB	0.62
Std. Error	0.020
Beta	0.628
t-statistics	9.117
F-statistics	72.520
Sig.	0.002
Adjusted R^2	0.483
Durbin-Watson Statistics	2.094

Note: DB = Digital Banking

The analysis revealed a significant positive relationship between these two factors. The coefficient for digital banking was 0.62 with a standard error of 0.020, indicating that a 1% increase in digital banking adoption corresponded to a 62% improvement in customer satisfaction quality. The beta value of 0.628 further confirmed this strong positive correlation. The t-statistic of 9.117 and an F-statistic of 72.520 with a p-value of 0.002 demonstrated the robustness of the overall estimate. The adjusted R-squared value of 0.483 suggested that 48% of the variation in customer satisfaction quality could be attributed to digital banking adoption, while the remaining 52% was explained by other factors not considered in the analysis. The Durbin-Watson statistic of 2.894 indicated no significant autocorrelation in the residuals. The descriptive statistics further supported these findings. Customers who frequently used digital banking unanimously agreed that it facilitated faster transactions at the bank's branch, with 57.1% strongly agreeing and 42.9% agreeing. Additionally, 90% of customers strongly agreed that digital banking saved time, with the remaining 10% partially agreeing. This unanimous agreement highlighted the time-saving benefits and enhanced service quality provided by digital banking. The inferential analysis corroborated these findings, indicating that increased digital banking adoption improved customer satisfaction with the services provided by GT Bank Liberia.

CONCLUSION: The study investigated the impact of digital banking on customer satisfaction quality and customer loyalty at GT Bank Liberia Limited. The findings of this study demonstrate a significant positive relationship between digital banking adoption and customer loyalty. Specifically, a 1% increase in digital banking adoption corresponded with 33% in Customer loyalty (p=0.000). This finding is consistent with previous studies that have demonstrated a link between digital banking and customer loyalty in the context of digital banking (Chiu et al., 2009; Singhal & Padhmanabhan, 2008). When customers perceive digital banking services as reliable, accurate, and error-free, it contributes to their overall satisfaction and fosters a sense of loyalty towards the bank (Uwalaka & Eze, 2020). For customer satisfaction quality, the result shows that a 1% increase in digital banking usage is associated with and 62% increase in customer satisfaction quality (p=0.002). This result aligns with previous research that has highlighted the positive impact of digital banking services on customer satisfaction (Akhtar et al., 2021; Umbas, 2017). The availability of convenient, efficient, and reliable digital banking channels has been shown to enhance customer experiences and perceptions of service quality (Bauer et al., 2005). The descriptive statistics further corroborated these findings, with the majority of customers agreeing that digital banking reduced errors, ensured successful transactions on the first attempt, and minimized website downtime. These factors contribute to perceived reliability and accuracy, which are crucial determinants of customer satisfaction and loyalty (Idowu & Fadiman, 2015). Moreover, almost all respondents acknowledged that the availability of digital banking services enhanced their loyalty to GT Bank Liberia Limited, reinforcing the positive relationship between digital banking adoption and customer loyalty. The findings of this study are in line with previous research, emphasizing the importance of digital banking in enhancing customer satisfaction and fostering customer loyalty in the banking sector.

Recommendations

Against this backdrop, the study recommends the following:

Enhancing digital infrastructure - The research highlights the positive impact of digital banking on customer satisfaction and loyalty. Therefore, it is recommended that GT Bank Liberia and other financial institutions in the country continue to invest in and improve their digital banking infrastructure. This may include upgrading systems, enhancing website performance, and ensuring seamless integration across various digital channels. A robust and reliable digital infrastructure can further enhance customer experiences and foster long-term loyalty. **Implementing personalized experiences -** As digital banking services become more ubiquitous, customers may expect personalized experiences tailored to their individual preferences and needs. Banks should explore ways to leverage customer data and analytics to offer customized services, personalized recommendations, and tailored communication. This can contribute to a more engaging and satisfying digital banking experience, subsequently strengthening customer loyalty. **Embracing omnichannel integration -** While the study emphasizes the benefits of digital banking, it is essential to recognize that customers may prefer a combination of digital and traditional channels. Banks should strive for seamless omnichannel integration, ensuring a consistent and cohesive experience across different touchpoints. This could involve integrating mobile apps, online banking platforms, and physical branch services, allowing customers to seamlessly switch between channels based on their preferences and needs. **Exploring emerging technologies** - The banking industry should stay abreast of emerging technologies and explore their potential applications in digital banking. This could include leveraging artificial intelligence, machine learning, and advanced analytics to enhance customer experiences, improve security measures, and provide personalized recommendations. Additionally, exploring the potential of blockchain technology, biometrics, and other innovative solutions could position banks at the forefront of digital transformation in the industry.

References

1. Antonio, F., Luz, N., Cruz, S., & Almeida, F. (2022). Digital marketing: A literature review on definitions, insights, and future trends. Journal of Theoretical and Applied Electronic Commerce Research, 17(7), 2837-2855.

2. Qian, C., Li, Z., & Zhao, S. (2023). Digital marketing for luxury brands in China: From the perspective of consumer experience. Journal of Marketing Analytics, 11(1), 21-34.

3. Idowu, P. A., & Fadiran, D. (2015). Adoption and use of digital banking services by customers of commercial banks in Nigeria. International Journal of Economic Behavior, 5(1), 1-16.

4.Umbas, N. (2017). The influence of digital banking services on customer satisfaction and loyalty: An empirical study in Indonesia. International Journal of Bank Marketing, 35(6), 949-971.

5.Uwalaka, S. K., & Eze, R. C. (2020). Digital banking, customer satisfaction, and bank performance: Evidence from Nigeria. International Journal of Financial Studies, 8(3), 45.

6.Akhtar, N., Khan, M. S., & Khan, M. M. (2021). Digital banking and customer satisfaction in the banking industry of Pakistan. Journal of Internet Banking and Commerce, 26(4), 1-16.

7.Bauer, H. H., Hammerschmidt, M., & Falk, T. (2005). Measuring the quality of e-banking portals. International Journal of Bank Marketing, 23(2), 153-175.

8.Chiu, C. M., Lin, H. Y., Sun, S. Y., & Hsu, M. H. (2009). Understanding customers' loyalty intentions towards online shopping: an integration of technology acceptance model and fairness theory. Behaviour & Information Technology, 28(4), 347-360.

4. Policy to Practice: Implementing sustainable port infrastructure.

S M Faiyaz Hossain Rashad

Global Logistics and Supply chain Management

University of Tasmania, 13 Monash Street, Mowbray 7248 Launceston, Tasmania **Australia**

Abstract: One of the most important initiatives to reduce the environmental effects of marine activity is the transition of port infrastructure towards sustainability. This article explores how policy concepts are translated into real-world implementations in the context of creating sustainable port infrastructures. At the operational level, we investigate the relationships that exist between international policies, national plans, and real practices. The emphasis is on how regional policies like the European Green Deal and global mandates like the International Maritime Organization (IMO) are implemented in ports as practical procedures. A review of current policy frameworks highlights a robust set of guidelines aimed at reducing greenhouse gas emissions and enhancing energy efficiency. However, the implementation of these policies at the port level encounters various challenges, including technological limitations, financial constraints, and the need for stakeholder alignment. To address these issues, this paper examines case studies from leading ports that have successfully integrated sustainability into their operations, such as the Ports of Rotterdam and Singapore. These examples demonstrate effective strategies such as the adoption of shore power technology, operational adjustments for reducing idle times, and the implementation of advanced logistics systems. Further, we analyse the role of technological innovation and collaboration among port authorities, shipping companies, and governments in fostering a sustainable transformation. The findings suggest that while significant progress has been made, gaps remain in achieving uniformity across different regions and scales of port operations. The paper concludes with recommendations for enhancing policy coherence and promoting broader adoption of best practices, emphasizing the critical need for a synergistic approach between policymaking and ground-level execution to achieve sustainable port infrastructure. This study contributes to the ongoing discussion on maritime sustainability, offering insights into the complexities of implementing policy in a diverse and globally interconnected industry.

Keywords: Sustainable infrastructure, port development, environmental policy, green ports, Port Operations

Introduction

Maritime shipping remains one of the most important modes of transport with ports being the focal points in the overall trade. Nevertheless, ports generate pollution that affects both micro and macro communities within the globe. Thus, to address the issue, there is the recent international and national policies that seek to enhance sustainability and curb emissions of greenhouse gases (GHG) within ports. This paper looks at the alignment of policy goals and practices regarding sustainable port infrastructure as one of its objectives. It investigates how global guidelines on the topic, for example, the guidelines by the International Maritime Organization (IMO), and local-continental framework, for instance, the European Green Deal (EGD), are implemented into measures within ports. Consequently, analysis aims at understanding the best practices for the implementation of such policies as well as the challenges faced in practice to realise sustainable operation of ports.

Research Background

Universal demand for sustainable port infrastructure is on the rise due to increased environmental degradation in ports. Seaports are also a source of air and water pollution and are sources of noise and habitat disruption to the communities and the environment (Notteboom & Lam (2020). United Nations SDG 14 is specifically related to conserving oceans, seas and marine resources for sustainable use (United Nations, 2021). According to these goals, the IMO has put in place goals of reducing of GHG emissions from international shipping by at least 50% in 2050 from the 2008 baseline (IMO, 2021).

However, these measures indicate that the practical application of sustainable technology and practices is still a severe obstacle in the ports. The use of such options as the utilization of alternative fuels, shore power and digital technologies implies substantial investment and joint actions of many subjects. Furthermore, there is the aspect of a difference in the economic statuses of ports across the globe, which creates another challenge to the implementational process (Patel & Jackson, 2022).

Discussions

Policy Frameworks

International Policies: The IMO's Initial Strategy on the emission control of GHS identifying the target of decreasing the shipping industry's carbon intensity by at least 40% by 2030 and aiming for peak overall CO2 emissions from international shipping as soon possible (IMO, 2021). This strategy contains a vision to hence, link the goal of the Paris Agreement to the maritime industry and re-emphasize the need for equal effort all over the world in achieving low emission in the industry. The European Green Deal outlines EU's plan for a climate-neutral economy by 2050 while boosting sustainability in different sectors, including maritime transport as highlighted in the EU's EU Strategy for the Sustainable and Competitive Aviation Industry (European Commission, 2023). The EGD also centres on policy instruments, subsidies, financial carrots and other encouragement of research and development. **National Strategies:** Currently, the United States Environmental Protection Agency or EPA has established the Ports Initiative, which aims to decrease air pollution as well as promote better goals and policies for sustainable ports through additional financing and technical support (EPA, 2022). It should assign green ports as one of the state development priorities, using options such as shore power, LNG and other clean energy sources (Ministry of Transport of China, 2022). Currently, European ports including Scandinavian countries like Norway and Sweden have progressive policies towards zero-emission controlled berthing by 2030 with sufficient government support and PDA participation (Hansen & Larsen, 2022).**Industry Practices: Renewable Energy Applications:** Solar and wind energy technologies are increasingly being promoted as sustainable options to the more conventional sources of power such as those dependent on non-renewable sources in port environments (Yang el al., 2023). The major ports of Rotterdam and Singapore are already setting scenarios for adopting the use of renewable energy sources to support their operations. **Digital Transformation:** Computerization and the knowledge of the new innovative ways of managing ports is ongoing. Real-time tracking, forecasting, and process controls are improving productivity, risk management, and situational eco-friendliness (Lee, Song, & Jang, 2021). That way, through the digital transformation, ports are now capable of managing resources and cutting down their emission levels. **Effective Governance:** The actions of large corporations and their interactions with other relevant actors need to be planned and managed to enhance sustainable management practices. There is a clear example of global ports such as Gothenburg in Sweden that have created partnerships to facilitate the development of honoring relationships with multiple stakeholders like the government, shipping organizations, technology companies, and the public (Gothenburg Port Authority, 2023). This adds knowledge to the pool, resources and coordination with special focus towards sustainability in the world Challenges. Although the situation has improved in recent years, there remain the following issues in the establishment of sustainable infrastructure for the seaport. Some of the challenges, which can be seen in the context of implementing sustainable solutions include high initial investments and risks related to technological innovation (Song & Panayides, 2021). The study by Patel and Jackson (2022) further shows that many smaller ports particularly from the developing states struggle to secure the required capital and resources which underlines the critical need for better and increased subsidization and incentive initiatives from the state and the intergovernmental institutions.

Findings and Results

Adoption of Shore Power Technology: Shore power technology, sometimes referred to as cold ironing, is an innovative system that enables ships to draw electrical current while being connected to a dock, thereby producing a cut off the emissions from the auxiliary engines. The following are the benefits of the specific technology used in oceans and seas: Local emission reductions: several ports that have adopted this technology have recorded significant decreases in local air pollution and the GHG emissions (Van Dyke & Mohammed, 2023).

Shore power technology and emission

Port	Emission Reduction (%)	Source
Rotterdam	40%	Van Dyke & Mohammed, 2023
Los Angeles	50%	Johnson & Lee, 2023
Singapore	30%	Chen, 2022

Figure 1.1 provides an overview on the actual emissions savings that ports, which invest in shore power technology, have been able to realize. Shift Towards Alternative Fuels: Regarding this, the reduction of emissions, especially by using other energy sources such as LNGs and biofuels, are helpful in minimizing the impact on maritime operations. For example, the Port of Singapore has paid close attention to energy savings and reduction of emissions by incorporating green technologies and even through the use of various forms of energy sources (Chen, 2022). Integration of Digital Technologies: Digital technologies are equally indispensable in the context of ports where they contribute to making work more effective and minimizing pollution. **The result indicated that the implementation of these**

underlying technologies for real-time monitoring and operational optimisation would bring about profound environmental improvements (Lee et al. , 2021). Efficiency and emissions reduction through digital technologies.

Technology	Efficiency Improvement (%)	Emission Reduction (%)	Source
Real-time Monitoring	20%	15%	Lee et al., 2021
Predictive Analytics	25%	18%	Van Dyke & Mohammed, 2023
Operational Optimization	30%	20%	Lee et al., 2021

Figure 1.2 shows the aspects of this approach that have helped to enhance port efficiency and emissions reduction through digital technologies. Financial Constraints: This indicates that the lack of adequate funds is one of the important issues that delay the implementation of sustainable technologies especially among the smaller ports. Challenges such as lack of access to finance, political instability and inadequate skills policies from governments and global organizations require increased financial commitment and incentives.

Discussion

Shore power system is effective, particularly in cutting emissions from vessels that are berthed at the particular terminals. The technology has benefits in decreasing local air pollution and GHG emissions where it has been applied and it is in line with the sustainability goals of the global community (Van Dyke & Mohammed, 2023). Change to other fuels some of which includes Liquefied Natural Gas (LNG) and biofuels has also helped to reduce the emission of carbon in transporting goods across the world. Singapore's case shows how willing polices and infrastructure investments are vital in support of such changes (Chen, 2022). Recent advancements in the digital technologies are changing the ways ports are managed, allowing monitoring, analysis, and optimization of their operations in real time. These technologies improve productivity, safety and reduce the impacts of the environment in the maritime business and at the same time encourage innovation as well as competition in the sector (Lee et al. , 2021). The use of technology in the port demonstrates positive impacts on the primary business processes and sustainability goals. Nevertheless, the issue of finances still persists as one of the primary reasons as to why sustainable technologies are not implemented. This is even more apparent in the current global environment, with smaller ports struggling with the challenges of obtaining the necessary capital and resources, which is why governments and international organizations need to improve financial aid and motivation programs (Patel & Jackson, 2022). Most often this is achieved through the cooperation of the port authorities, shipping companies, government and other contributors to sustainability plans. Programs such as the Global Industry Alliance to Support Low Carbon Shipping raise awareness of the synergistic efforts (Singh & Gupta, 2022). **Future**

Scope: Enhanced Policy Coherence: There is a need to harmonize international, national, and local policies to ensure consistent and effective implementation of sustainable practices. Enhanced policy coherence can help streamline efforts and resources towards achieving sustainability goals. **Technological Innovation:** Continued investment in and development of new technologies are essential to improve energy efficiency and reduce emissions in port operations. Emerging technologies, such as hydrogen fuel cells and advanced renewable energy systems, hold promise for further reducing the environmental impact of ports. **Financial Support:** Increased financial incentives and financing mechanisms can support those smaller ports, who lack sufficient resources and skills for providing to a full extent, to adopt sustainable practices. This requires that governments and international institutions target funding and technical assistance to get green technologies to a wide number of developing countries. **Stakeholder Collaboration:** Important to build a better partnership between the government agencies, port authorities, shipping companies, and the local communities to promote sustainability measures. Collaborative Platforms facilitate knowledge sharing, resource mobilization and collective action and coordination around common agendas. **Research and Development:** More research needs to be performed on the usage of emerging technologies and best practices will also help make port infrastructure more sustainable on an on-going basis. Research Towards Collaborative Initiatives. **Conclusion**

Sustainable port infrastructure is a complex and varied subject that calls for coordinated efforts from several stakeholders to go from policy to reality. This study emphasizes how crucial it is to have strong legislative frameworks, financial assistance, innovative technology, and stakeholder cooperation to promote sustainable growth in port infrastructure. The results show that ports all around the world are implementing sustainable practices at an increasing rate in order to lower carbon emissions and improve energy efficiency. But there are still major obstacles to overcome, such large upfront expenses and economic inequality. As we move forward, achieving the goal of carbon-neutral ports and robust supply chains requires encouraging innovation, investment, and cooperation. Through the establishment of policy-practice bridges, ports may mitigate their environmental effect and advance global sustainability objectives.

Glossary: GHG: Greenhouse Gas, IMO: International Maritime Organization, EGD: European Green Deal, SDG: Sustainable Development Goals, LNG: Liquefied Natural Gas, EPA: Environmental Protection Agency

References

1.Chen, S. (2022). Implementation of biofuels in Asian ports. *Journal of Green Maritime Technology, 12*(2), 34-48.

2.Environmental Protection Agency (EPA). (2022). *Ports Initiative.* Retrieved from https://www.epa.gov/ports-initiative

3. European Commission. (2023). *Europe's Green Deal and maritime implications*. Retrieved from https://ec.europa.eu/clima/eu-action/european-green-deal_en

4. Gothenburg Port Authority. (2023). *Sustainable Port*. Retrieved from https://www.portofgothenburg.com/sustainability/sustainable-port

5. Hansen, A., & Larsen, T. (2022). Denmark's maritime decarbonization strategy. *Scandinavian Journal of Environmental Law, 6*(2), 142-158.

6. International Maritime Organization. (2021). *IMO's GHG strategy*. Retrieved from http://imo.org

7. Johnson, S., & Lee, K. (2023). Local initiatives in decarbonizing ports: Cases from the US and China. *Environmental Management Journal, 11*(1), 45-59.

8. Lee, J., Song, D. W., & Jang, H. S. (2021). Enhancing port environmental sustainability through digital transformation: A review and future research directions. *Sustainability, 13*(9), 5192. https://doi.org/10.3390/su13095192

9. Ministry of Transport of the People's Republic of China. (2022). *Guidelines for Green Port Development*. Retrieved from http://www.mot.gov.cn

10. Notteboom, T., & Lam, J. S. L. (2020). Toward green ports: A study of the relationship between port authority governance and environmental performance. *Journal of Environmental*

Planning   and   Management,   63(8),   1375-1393. https://doi.org/10.1080/09640568.2019.1680960

11. Patel, S., & Jackson, R. (2022). Financial barriers to sustainable port infrastructure. *Journal of Maritime Economics & Logistics, 24*(4), 321-336. https://doi.org/10.1057/s41278-022-00201-4

12. Singh, R., & Gupta, A. (2022). Global Industry Alliance activities for low carbon shipping. *International Journal of Maritime Engineering, 14*(3), 206-219. https://doi.org/10.1007/s40722-021-00195-2

13. Song, D. W., & Panayides, P. M. (2021). The green port paradox: Factors affecting environmental management in ports. *Journal   of   Cleaner   Production,   312,* 127773. https://doi.org/10.1016/j.jclepro.2021.127773

14. United Nations. (2021). *Sustainable Development Goals.* Retrieved from https://sdgs.un.org/goals

15. Van Dyke, M., & Mohammed, A. (2023). Shore power and hybrid systems in European ports. *Energy Solutions for Sustainability, 17*(3), 134-148.

16. Yang, Z., Peng, Y., & Yuan, J. (2023). Renewable energy applications in seaports: A review of technologies and practices. *Sustainability,   15*(3), 2108. https://doi.org/10.3390/su15032108

5. Edge Computing and Artificial Intelligence: Revolutionizing Machine Learning from the Edge.

Ridhima Sehgal

Assistant Professor, Dept of Computer Applications, T John College, **India**

Abstract: Recent years have witnessed a huge recognition of the Internet of Things (IoT). By imparting sufficient information for version schooling and inference, IoT has promoted the improvement of artificial intelligence (AI) to an exceptional quantity. Under this background and trend, the conventional cloud computing model may also stumble upon many issues in independently tackling the big facts generated by IoT and the assembly of corresponding sensible wishes. In reaction, a new computing model called Edge computing has drawn good sized at both enterprise and academia. With the non-stop deepening of the research on Edge Computing (EC), students have discovered that conventional (non-AI) strategies have their barriers in enhancing the overall performance of EC. Seeing successful software of AI in diverse fields, EC researchers begin to set their points of interest on AI, specifically from a perspective of device studying, a branch of AI that has received multiplied popularity in the past long time. In this newsletter, we first explain the formal definition of EC and why EC has become a favorable computing model. Then, we speak about the issues of interest in EC.

Keywords: Edge AI, part computing, synthetic intelligence, real-time processing, IoT, clever towns, self-reliant structures, healthcare, business IoT

Introduction

In the evolving virtual landscape, two pivotal generations, Edge Computing and Artificial Intelligence (AI), are revolutionizing how information is processed, analyzed, and applied. Now Imagine a world where intelligence is not limited to massive statistics facilities and far-off clouds, but instead, it resides right at the threshold of our fingertips. Picture a state of affairs wherein data is processed and decisions are made instantly, revolutionizing industries and transforming our day-by-day lives. That's in which Edge Computing and Machine Learning come into play, operating hand in hand to revolutionize the manner we procedure, examine, and make choices with facts. Edge Computing, an allotted computing paradigm, brings the power of records processing towards the supply, decreasing latency and enabling actual-time insights. Meanwhile, Machine Learning, a subset of artificial intelligence, empowers computer systems to learn from records and make intelligent predictions without specific programming. Together, they shape a powerful alliance, unleashing the ability for localized intelligence, enhanced privateness, optimized bandwidth, and advanced device efficiency [1] **The Rise of Edge**

Computing : Proximity to Data: Edge computing devices, such as IoT sensors and gateways, are placed closer to the source of data, minimizing latency and enabling faster decision-making. Reduced Bandwidth Demands: By processing data at the edge, the need for constant data transmission to the cloud is reduced, optimizing network bandwidth utilization[2] Improved Privacy and Security: With sensitive data processed locally, edge computing enhances privacy and data security by limiting the exposure of sensitive information.[3] **Need of Edge Computing to Edge AI:** Edge computing and Edge AI are closely related concepts that build on each other to enhance the performance, efficiency, and capabilities of distributed computing systems. Here's a breakdown of the need for edge computing in the context of Edge AI: **Low Latency and Real-Time Processing Immediate Decision-Making:** Edge AI applications, such as autonomous vehicles, industrial robots, and real-time video analytics, require immediate processing and response times. By processing data at the edge (closer to the source), latency is significantly reduced, enabling real-time decision-making. Use Case Example: An autonomous vehicle cannot afford the delay of sending data to a remote cloud server for processing. Edge computing ensures that the vehicle can process sensor data on the spot and make split-second decisions. [4] **Bandwidth Efficiency:** Reduced Data Transmission: Edge computing reduces the need to send large volumes of raw data to centralized cloud servers. This is particularly important in scenarios where bandwidth is limited or expensive. Use Case Example: In a smart city environment, thousands of sensors generate data continuously.[5] Edge AI processes this data locally, transmitting only the most critical insights to the cloud, thereby conserving bandwidth. **Scalability and Flexibility**: Distributed Processing: Edge computing allows for the distribution of processing power across various edge devices, leading to better scalability. Each edge device can independently handle its own data processing needs, reducing the load on centralized systems. Use Case Example: In an IoT network of smart home devices, each device can independently process data and perform tasks, making the system more scalable and flexible. **Enhanced Privacy and Security Local Data Processing:** By keeping data processing local, edge computing helps protect sensitive information. Data is not transmitted over potentially insecure networks, reducing the risk of interception and breaches. Use Case Example: Healthcare applications, such as remote patient monitoring, can process sensitive health data on local devices, ensuring patient privacy and compliance with regulations like HIPAA. [6] **Improved Reliability and Resilience Reduced Dependency on Centralized Cloud**: Edge computing enhances the reliability and resilience of systems by reducing dependency on centralized cloud services, which may experience downtime or connectivity issues. Use Case Example: In remote or critical environments (e.g., oil rigs, space missions), edge devices can continue to operate and make decisions even if connectivity to the central cloud is lost. **Energy Efficiency Optimized Resource Utilization:** Edge computing can be more energy-efficient by reducing the need for continuous data transmission to the cloud and leveraging local processing capabilities. Use Case Example: Smart grids can use edge computing to optimize energy distribution and consumption in real time, reducing overall energy usage. Conclusion Edge computing is crucial for the effective deployment of Edge AI, addressing challenges related to latency, bandwidth, scalability, privacy, security, reliability, and energy efficiency. By processing data closer to the source, Edge AI systems can perform faster, more efficient, and more secure computations, enabling a wide range of applications that require real-time processing and decision-making.[7] **Edge AI: E**dge AI combines Artificial Intelligence and side computing. The AI algorithms are run on gadgets able to facet computing. The advantage of that is that the facts may be processed in actual time, while not having to connect with a cloud. Most cutting facet AI techniques are accomplished in a cloud as they mandate a huge quantity of computing energy. The result is that those AI procedures can be vulnerable to downtime. Because Edge AI systems operate on an area computing tool, vital statistics operations can arise domestically, being dispatched whilst an internet connection is hooked up, which saves time. The deep mastering algorithms can perform at the tool itself, the foundation factor of the records. Edge AI is becoming more and more important because of the reality that increasingly devices need to employ AI in conditions wherein they can't get admission to the cloud. Consider how many manufacturing unit robots or how many vehicles nowadays include laptop imaginative and prescient algorithms. A lag time in the transmission of data in those conditions could be catastrophic. Self-driving automobiles cannot suffer from latency while detecting items on the road. Since a quick response time is so essential, the tool itself should have an Edge AI gadget that lets it investigate and classify pix without counting on a cloud connection. When area computers are entrusted with the data processing duties commonly accomplished at the cloud, the result is actual-time low latency, actual-time processing. Additionally, using proscribing the transmission of statistics to simply the maximum important records, the statistics extent itself may be decreased and conversation interruptions may be minimized.

How Edge AI Works : Edge AI gadgets use system learning algorithms to screen the device's behavior and collect and system the tool statistics. These algorithms can run at once at the brink of a given network, near where the facts and information needed to run the system are generated, consisting of an IoT tool or system ready with an aspect computing device. This permits the tool to make choices, routinely correct problems, and predict destiny performance.

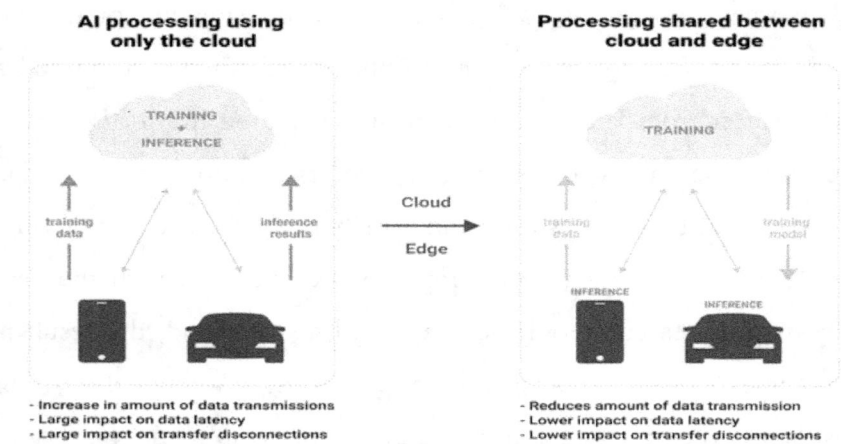

Fig 1:AI using Cloud /AI using Cloud and Edge [10]

The uncertainty in selecting among Edge AI and Cloud AI commonly happens for system studying or deep mastering use instances. As deep studying algorithms require intensive processing hence the performance of the hardware turns into a massive aspect. Cloud AI can truly offer better performance for the machine, but most deep mastering applications cannot compromise with latency in information transfer and the security threats within the community. Hence, Edge AI outlives Cloud AI for synthetic intelligence packages. As mentioned earlier, the strength consumption element constantly intervenes in Edge AI processors. It is comprehensible as heavy computations require a better energy delivery. However the cutting-edge Edge AI processors have AI accelerators that provide higher performance with low electricity intake. However, GPUs and TPUs nevertheless require higher strength, but the improvements in design and circuit structure will overpower this issue. **Machine Learning At The Edge**

Embedded ML Models: Edge devices can host compact, efficient machine learning models that can perform inference tasks locally, reducing the need for cloud-based processing. **Federated Learning:** This collaborative approach to training AI models allows edge devices to contribute to the model's development while preserving data privacy and security. **Continual Learning:** Edge AI systems can continuously adapt and learn from new data, enabling them to evolve and improve their performance over time. **On-Device Training:** Some edge devices can even perform model training directly on the device, further reducing the need for centralized processing and data transmission.

AI at the Edge: Unleashing the Potential

https://thirdeyedata.ai/significance-and-applications-of-edge-ai/

Real-Time Responsiveness Combining edge computing and AI allows intelligent systems to respond to events and make decisions instantaneously, enabling time-critical applications like autonomous vehicles and smart manufacturing. **Distributed Intelligence** Edge AI allows for distributed, collaborative intelligence, where devices can share insights and work together to solve complex problems, improving overall system resilience. **Energy Efficiency**Performing AI computations at the edge can significantly reduce the energy consumption associated with data transmission and cloud-based processing, making edge AI systems more sustainable. **Security Cameras:** Security cameras generate a substantial volume of data continuously, spanning minutes, hours, and days. This data is predominantly in video format, resulting in significantly larger file sizes compared to other sensor-generated data. To mitigate these issues, Edge AI is employed. With this paradigm, cameras are endowed with autonomous processing capabilities. They continuously generate data in smaller, more manageable chunks through object detection, image/frame classification, pedestrian detection, and Optical Character Recognition (OCR) for discerning vehicle number plates of those infringing traffic regulations. The cameras process this data at the edge device level, intelligently discarding extraneous information. Only pertinent data is forwarded to the server or designated storage medium, such as cloud storage. This streamlined approach substantially reduces payload sizes, resulting in many benefits. These include lower latency, and less bandwidth usage, which in turn facilitates the integration of additional applications within the existing bandwidth allocation. Furthermore, it leads to reduced storage costs, heightened reliability, and mitigated privacy and security risks.**Intelligent Home Appliances:** Home appliances like Smart Speakers, Smart thermostats, etc. All of these devices process the generated data at the edge device level like – Smart Speakers – These employ edge AI to interpret the voice messages or the speech locally not depending solely on the cloud architecture.**Manufacturing Robots:** Robots in the factories use Edge AI to adapt to different tasks, analyze machine health in real time, and predict maintenance needs, reducing potential downtimes.**Retail Analytics Systems:** These systems use Edge AI to analyze customer behavior in real time, enabling personalized marketing and real-time inventory management.**Mobile Healthcare Applications:**In mobile healthcare applications, Edge AI enables real-time monitoring of vital signs, such as heart rate and blood pressure, using wearable devices. This allows for immediate health insights and alerts, enhancing patient care and well-being while minimizing the need for constant connectivity to a central server.**Drones for Agricultural Monitoring:** Drones equipped with Edge AI technology navigate and analyze farms, identifying areas that need water, fertilizer, or pest control. Operating area AI in the discipline requires numerous considerations: **Security:** Edge AI devices may incorporate touchy facts or be accountable for important capabilities, so it's vital to put into effect facts security measures to shield them from cyber threats. This can consist of facts encryption, getting the right of entry to controls, and software updates to deal with safety vulnerabilities. **Monitoring and protection**: Edge AI gadgets might also require tracking and upkeep to make sure their continued operation. This can encompass tracking for hardware screw-ups, software bugs, and connectivity troubles, and scheduling normal preservation to deal with these issues. In addition, there may be a want to monitor predictions from the AI version and evaluate their accuracy and relevance, because AI models are acknowledged to degrade in performance through the years (a phenomenon known as data flow). **Connectivity**: Edge AI gadgets require community connectivity to talk with other devices, ship information, and acquire updates. In faraway areas or harsh environments, connectivity can be constrained or unreliable, so it's vital to select side devices that can function offline and sync information while connectivity is to be had. **Power**

consumption: Edge gadgets may additionally function on battery energy, sun power, or different opportunity strength assets, so it's essential to pick devices that are optimized for low power consumption. This may be completed via hardware optimizations, consisting of the usage of low-energy processors, or through software program optimizations, inclusive of lowering the frequency of facts transmissions. [8-9] **Environmental factors:** Edge AI devices may be deployed in harsh environments, consisting of extreme temperatures, humidity, or vibration. It's critical to choose gadgets that are designed to operate in these conditions and are resilient to environmental factors that could impact their overall performance. **6. Privacy-Preserving Techniques:** Ensuring that data privacy is maintained while processing on side devices: Differential Privacy: Techniques that add noise to records or fashions to make sure personal records factors can't be reverse-engineered. Secure Enclaves: Hardware-primarily based protection capabilities that ensure sensitive computations are isolated from the relaxation of the machine. 7. **Real-Time Processing Techniques:** Optimizing for low-latency and real-time AI programs: Pipeline Parallelism: Dividing a model into exclusive tiers that can be processed in parallel to reduce latency. Edge Caching: Storing often used records or model outputs locally to reduce processing time. **The Future of Edge AI:** With advancing generations, Edge AI algorithms are poised to address complicated duties with exceptional performance. The convergence of factors like neural community adulthood, IoT proliferation, and 5G generation leads us into a brand-new era, putting the level for businesses in each area to seamlessly integrate AI and use real-time insights to enhance operations throughout sectors. The destiny of Edge AI holds terrific promise, bringing innovations so one can reshape industries and gasoline remarkable growth.

Conclusion

In precis, Edge computing is crucial for the effective deployment of Edge AI, addressing challenges related to latency, bandwidth, scalability, privacy, security, reliability, and energy efficiency. By processing data closer to the source, Edge AI systems can perform faster, more efficient, and more secure computations, enabling a wide range of applications that require real-time processing and decision-making.

References

[1] K. Cao, Y. Liu, G. Meng and Q. Sun, "An Overview on Edge Computing Research," in *IEEE Access*, vol. 8, pp. 85714-85728, 2020, Doi: 10.1109/ACCESS.2020.2991734.

[2] Rhea, Sarah & Kibona, Tito & Dipaola, Daniella & Nugent, Julia & Alemdar, Meltem & Zhong, Ying & Hansen, Justin & Zang, Wenston & Nguyen, Tan & Klopfenstein, Nathan & Flynn, Leslie & Bashar, MD & Jaiswal, Palashkumar & Simons-Linares, Roberto & Sandhu, Simran & Kandwal, Pankaj & Tomić, Vajdana & Karandikar, Sharad & Lunevicius, Raimundas. (2024). The Rise of edge computing: changing the way we process data.

https://www.researchgate.net/publication/379370338_The_rise_of_e
dge_computing_changing_the_way_we_process_data.

[3] T. Wang, J. Zhou, X. Chen, G. Wang, A. Liu, Y. Liu, A three-layer privacy-preserving cloud storage scheme based on computational intelligence in fog computing, IEEE Transactions on Emerging Topics in Computational Intelligence 2 (1) (2018) 3–12.

[4] Y. -L. Lee, P. -K. Tsung and M. Wu, "Techology trend of edge AI," *2018 International Symposium on VLSI Design, Automation and Test (VLSI-DAT)*, Hsinchu, Taiwan, 2018, pp. 1-2, doi: 10.1109/VLSI-DAT.2018.8373244.

[5] Deng, Shuiguang & Zhao, Hailiang & Fang, Weijia & Yin, Jianwei & Dustdar, Schahram & Zomaya, Albert. (2019). Edge Intelligence: The Confluence of Edge Computing and Artificial Intelligence.
https://www.researchgate.net/publication/335650663_Edge_Intellige
nce_The_Confluence_of_Edge_Computing_and_Artificial_Intelligenc
e

 [6] L. Zhang, J. Li, Enabling robust and privacy-preserving resource allocation in fog computing, IEEE Access 6 (2018) 50384–50393.

[7] L. Gu, D. Zeng, S. Guo, A. Barnawi, Y. Xiang, Cost efficient resource management in fog computing supported medical cyber-physical system, IEEE Transactions on Emerging Topics in Computing 5 (1) (2017) 108–119.

[8} Hao C., Qin Y., and Hua H.. 2020. Energy "routers," "computers," and "protocols." In *Energy Internet: Systems and Applications*. Springer Nature Switzerland AG, 193–208

[9] Liang H., Hua H., Qin Y., Ye M., Zhang S., and Cao J.. 2022. Stochastic optimal energy storage management for energy routers via compressive sensing. *IEEE Trans. Ind. Inform.* 18, 4 (2022) 2192–2202.

.

6. AI-Driven Optimization of Inventory Systems: A Comprehensive ABC Analysis Approach.

Dr. Animesh Kumar Sharma

Assistant Professor & HOD, Faculty of Science and technology, The ICFAI University Raipur, **India**

Abstract: This research study introduces a new method to enhance inventory control by combining Artificial Intelligence (AI) methods with the ABC analysis approach. The research examines the possible advantages of using AI algorithms to improve the precision and effectiveness of inventory categorization and distribution. By merging AI-powered predictive analytics with conventional ABC analysis, companies can enhance inventory management; lower carrying expenses, and boost operational efficiency. The study discusses how AI-powered solutions can be used in inventory management practices, including the methodology, findings, and implications.

Keywords: artificial intelligence, inventory management, abc analysis, optimization, predictive analytics, inventory control, decomposition algorithms, inventory shortages, automatic classification, professional class, pareto distribution, inventory items

Introduction

Inventory management is a critical component of supply chain management, encompassing controlling and supervising goods and materials. Efficient inventory management ensures that a business maintains optimal stock levels to meet customer demand without incurring unnecessary costs. Traditional methods often need to be revised to address modern supply chains' complexities. Recent advancements in artificial intelligence (AI) offer new opportunities for optimizing inventory systems, mainly through enhanced methods such as ABC analysis. This chapter explores the integration of AI in inventory management, focusing on its application to ABC analysis, and highlights the potential improvements in efficiency and accuracy.

Description of Study: The study aims to optimize inventory systems using AI-driven ABC analysis. ABC analysis is a well-known categorization method that classifies inventory items into three categories—A, B, and C—based on their importance. Category A includes high-value items with low sales frequency, category B consists of moderate-value items with moderate sales frequency, and category C comprises low-value items with high sales frequency. By leveraging AI, the study seeks to refine this classification process, making it more dynamic and accurate.

Data was collected from various industries to evaluate the effectiveness of AI algorithms in enhancing traditional ABC analysis. The study involved applying machine learning models to inventory data, focusing on improving decision-making processes and reducing costs associated with inventory management.

Novelty of Study: This study introduces a novel approach integrating AI with traditional inventory management techniques. The combination of AI and ABC analysis offers a comprehensive and data-driven method for inventory categorization. Unlike traditional ABC analysis, which relies on static thresholds and manual calculations, AI-driven ABC analysis uses advanced algorithms to dynamically assess inventory data, leading to more accurate and timely classifications.

The innovative aspect of this study lies in its ability to transform inventory systems through AI-driven insights. AI algorithms can quickly process large volumes of data and identify patterns that may not be apparent through manual analysis. This capability allows for more precise forecasting, better resource allocation, and improved inventory management efficiency.

Concept of Inventory Systems

Inventory systems are designed to manage the procurement, storage, and distribution of goods. Effective inventory management ensures a business maintains the right stock balance to meet customer demand while minimizing costs. The critical components of inventory management include:

- **Procurement**: The process of sourcing and purchasing goods.
- **Storage**: The management of inventory within warehouses, ensuring efficient use of space and resources.
- **Distribution**: The logistics of delivering goods to customers promptly.

Traditional inventory management faces several challenges, such as overstocking, stockouts, and high carrying costs. These issues can lead to increased operational costs and reduced customer satisfaction. AI-driven inventory systems aim to address these challenges by providing more accurate forecasting, real-time data analysis, and automated decision-making processes.

Review of ABC Analysis

ABC analysis is a widely used inventory categorization method that segments inventory items into three classes based on their importance. This method helps prioritize management efforts and resources toward the most critical items.

- **Class A Items**: These are high-value items with low sales frequency, accounting for a significant portion of the inventory value but a small portion of the total inventory quantity.
- **Class B Items**: These items have a moderate value and sales frequency, representing a balanced approach to inventory management.
- **Class C Items**: Low-value items with high sales frequency comprise most of the inventory quantity but a small portion of the inventory value.

The primary benefits of ABC analysis include improved inventory control, better resource allocation, and enhanced efficiency in managing stock levels. Businesses can maintain optimal inventory levels and minimize costs by focusing on the most critical items.

Need of ABC Analysis

ABC analysis is essential for effective inventory management for several reasons:

- **Inventory Control**: ABC analysis helps identify the most critical items that require close monitoring and control, ensuring that high-value items are always available to meet customer demand.

- **Cost Management**: Businesses can optimize stock levels and reduce carrying costs by categorizing inventory items based on their importance. It helps prevent overstocking and stockouts, leading to cost savings and improved cash flow.

- **Resource Allocation**: ABC analysis enables businesses to allocate resources more effectively, focusing on the most essential items. It ensures that management efforts are directed toward the items that impact the business most.

- **Foundation for Advanced Strategies**: ABC analysis provides a foundation for implementing more sophisticated inventory management techniques, such as just-in-time (JIT) inventory and economic order quantity (EOQ). These strategies can further enhance efficiency and reduce costs.

Methodology

The methodology of this study involves several key steps:

1. **Data Collection**: Inventory data, including sales records, purchase orders, and inventory logs, was collected from various industries to train and test the AI algorithms.

2. **AI Algorithms**: Machine learning models were applied to the inventory data to classify items into A, B, and C categories. The algorithms used include clustering, classification, and regression techniques.

3. **Data Preprocessing**: The collected data was cleaned and normalized to ensure accuracy and consistency. This step is crucial for improving the performance of the AI algorithms.

4. **Applying AI Models**: The AI algorithms were applied to the preprocessed data to classify inventory items. The results were then compared with traditional ABC analysis outcomes to evaluate improvements.

5. **Evaluation**: The effectiveness of AI-driven ABC analysis is measured in terms of cost savings, efficiency improvements, and accuracy of inventory categorization. The study assessed the results using various performance metrics, such as precision, recall, and F1-score.

This study uses AI to take a more dynamic and accurate approach to inventory classification. By leveraging machine learning models, the study aims to provide real-time insights and improve decision-making processes in inventory management.

Conclusion

The integration of AI with ABC analysis offers significant improvements in inventory management. The study demonstrates that AI-driven ABC analysis provides more accurate and efficient inventory categorization, leading to better resource allocation and cost savings.

By quickly processing large volumes of data and identifying patterns, AI can enhance forecasting, optimize stock levels, and reduce operational costs.

The findings of this study have important implications for businesses across various industries. Adopting AI-driven inventory systems can improve efficiency, reduce costs, and increase customer satisfaction. Future research should focus on refining AI models and exploring additional applications of AI in supply chain and inventory management.

References

[1]Veres, P. (2023). Increasing the efficiency of warehouse analysis using artificial intelligence. *Acta Logistica (AL)*, 10(3).

[2]Frank, E., & Henry, E. (2024). AI-Driven Demand Forecasting for Optimized Inventory Management (No. 13214). *EasyChair*.

[3]Svoboda, J., & Minner, S. (2022). Tailoring inventory classification to industry applications: the benefits of understandable machine learning. *International Journal of Production Research*, 60(1), 388-401.

[4]Miroedova, S. (2023). Thesis Study: analysis of the implementation of Artificial Intelligence in warehouses of e-commerce SMEs based on feasibility study.

[5]Pal, S. (2023). Advancements in AI-Enhanced Just-In-Time Inventory: Elevating Demand Forecasting Accuracy.

International Journal for Research in Applied Science & Engineering Technology, 11, 282-289.

[6]Bhattacharya, A., Sarkar, B., & Mukherjee, S. K. (2007). Distance-based consensus method for ABC analysis. *International Journal of Production Research*, 45(15), 3405-3420.

[7]Groenewald, E., & Kilag, O. K. (2024). E-commerce Inventory Auditing: Best Practices, Challenges, and the Role of Technology. *International Multidisciplinary Journal of Research for Innovation, Sustainability, and Excellence (IMJRISE)*, 1(2), 36-42.

[8]Mohammed, S. A., & Workneh, B. D. (2020). Critical analysis of pharmaceuticals inventory management using the ABC-VEN matrix in Dessie referral Hospital, Ethiopia. *Integrated Pharmacy Research and Practice*, 113-125.

[9]Larsen, C. (2021). Alignment between an ABC classification and results from an optimization approach. *INFOR: Information Systems and Operational Research*, 59(3), 400-410.

7. Preeminent Practices to Enrich Language Proficiency.

Bonisiwe Happiness Maphumulo

South Africa

Eudoxia Research Centre (ERC), India, Eudoxia Research University (ERU), USA

Abstract: According to the Curriculum and Assessment Policy Statement (CAPS), learning a second or additional language follows the same path as attaining home language, except that it occurs later in a child's life (Department of Basic Education, 2011). Nevertheless, an additional language requires a more cognizant effort than home language and therefore necessitates different and specific methodologies to be mastered successfully, hence this paper aims to unveil methodologies drawn from research to enrich language proficiency in learners doing English as First Additional Language. The paper is located within qualitative research approach which is underpinned by Interpretivism paradigm and case study as a research design. Information rich participants were purposively selected for data collection; teachers who have taught language for more than five years and learners who are doing English as First Additional Language. A sample of 4 educators and 6 learners in one selected primary school was used. Data was thereafter analyzed using thematic analysis.

Literature reveals that current methods are simply not moving EFAL learners to the level of proficiency that is expected of them. It also appears that teachers rely solely on traditional methods. To assists learners with limited English proficiency it is recommended that teachers make content comprehensible through the use of different pedagogies drawn from research to enrich proficiency and to ensure that these learners master content with success.

Keywords: preeminent, practices, proficiency, pedagogies

Introduction

Fluency and proficiency in language is essential in order to access higher education and enter the labour market (Taylor & von Fintel, 2016). In South Africa, this is no different. South Africa is a very diverse country culturally, socially and linguistically. This poses various challenges regarding education in our country, particularly the issue regarding second language acquisition and methods used to impart the content to learners (Steyn, 2017). The literature reveals that methods used to convey the content are outdated and they don't move learners to the level of language proficiency that is expected of them. The use of best practices drawn from reaserach is therefore paramount to enrich proficiency in EFAL leaners. It is without a doubt that the application of best methodologies will lay a solid foundation for successful academic performance in the future. Steyn, (2017) agrees with the above statement, a range of approaches, methodologies and strategies drawn from research must be used. One of them is the Cognitive Academic Language Learning Approach (CALLA). CALLA is an American programme that was developed to provide transitional instruction to further academic language development in English through content area instruction. CALLA uses English as a tool to learn subject matter. The objective of this model is to develop the academic language skills of learners with limited English proficiency. (Steyn, 2017) further states that CALLA can help EFAL learners in understanding and retaining content while they are increasing their English proficiency. **Theoretical Framework: Linguistic Theory:** Theoretical lenses adopted for the study was Linguistic theory as it deals with language properties. Linguistic theory was developed by Noam Chomsky in 1928 who is now known as the father of modern linguistics. Chomsky is a distinguished linguist who described language as a grammar that is largely independent of language use (Hosni, 2019). This theory argues that language acquisition is governed by universal, underlying grammatical rules that are common to all typically developing humans. This theory is not new and has been reviewed by many theorists. Linguistic theory came to be known in the late 19th Century by Neogrammarians. Neogrammarians examined sound alterations and sound laws which lead to sound change (Schmid, 2012). In the 20th Century, Structuralism was introduced by Ferninand de Saussure supplementing Neogrammarianism. Structuralists scrutinised language structure and sound image. Structuralists held that everything has meaning. In the late 20th Century, Post-structuralism emerged. It was introduced by Jacques Derrida. Post-structuralists built on critiques of Saussure's linguistic insights. Post-structuralists were of the view that grammar of a language has rules and structures. Years later Noam Chomsky introduced Generative Grammar which builds upon Post-structuralism. This model has been dominant formal linguistics and in recent decades. It has refined Linguistic theory. One of Chomsky's theoretical insights reveals that humans were born with a predisposition to learn the grammar of a language. Human beings are pre-wired to learn the grammar of a language, and are born with basic rules for language, intact (Hosni, 2019), Hosni is of the notion that the human brain is ready-made to acquire the grammar of a language quickly at specific stages in the development process.

Principles of Linguistic Theory: Phonology (study of speech sounds) Phonology is the branch of linguistics concerned with the study of speech sounds with reference to their distribution and patterning (Odden, 2013), the principles that govern the way sounds are organised in languages, and the variations that occur are explained. Phonology aims to analyse an individual language to determine which sound units are used and which pattern they form, and involve the comparison of the properties of different sound systems (Odden, 2013). Morphology (study of word formation) This branch examines the internal makeup and structure of words, as well as the patterns and principles underlying their composition (Schmid, 2015). Words are analysed in terms of morphemes (components of words that are carriers of meaning). The major areas of morphology are: inflectional morphology which deals with grammar; derivational morphology which is word formation which deals with patterns and rules guiding the formation of words. **Semantics (meaning of words and sentences)** This branch of linguistics studies the meaning of words and sentences (Oliveria, 2004). It is of the view that sentences should be meaningful and valid. Semantics largely determines grammar comprehension. One of the central issues with semantics is the distinction between literal and figurative meaning. Literal meaning takes the concept at face value while figurative utilizes similes and metaphors for example to represent meaning and convey greater emotion (Sasha, 2015). Syntax (rules of grammar with regards to sentence structure) This branch of linguistics involves the rules underlying the way words are arranged. Meaningfully. One cannot just place words in any order to make a meaningful sentence (Nuin, 2019). There are certain rules for making sentences e.g. the main device for showing relationships among words is word order: subject is the initial position, the verb then the object; transposing them changes the meaning. Syntax is a form of grammar concerned with the order of words in sentences.

Related Literature: According to the Curriculum and Assessment Policy Statement (CAPS), learning a second or additional language follows the same path as attaining a HL, except that it occurs later in a child's life (Department of Basic Education, 2011). Nevertheless, an additional language requires a more cognisant effort than the HL and therefore necessitates different and specific methodologies. CAPS (DBE, 2011) recommends the additive approach for teaching an additional language. This approach assumes that learners who start school are competent in their HL and that they can use their HL to learn an additional language. In order to master grammar successfully, a range of approaches, methodologies and strategies drawn from research must be used. One of them is the Cognitive Academic Language Learning Approach (CALLA), which is a content-based ESL model designed by Chamot and O'Malley as a "bridge to the mainstream" (Steyn, 2017). This instructional programme assists learners with limited English proficiency in the transition to mainstream instruction in English by making content comprehensible through the use of English for Speakers of Other Languages (ESOL) strategies and teaching EFAL learners how to handle content area material with success. Other approaches drawn from research that are regarded as the best in enhancing grammar accuracy are Presentation-Practice-Production (PPP) model and the integration of the Fourth Industrial Revolution. All three approaches will be discussed as to how they are of paramount in enhancing grammar in EFAL learners

Cognitive Academic Language Learning Approach (CALLA)

CALLA is an American programme that was developed to provide transitional instruction to further academic language development in English through content area instruction. Instead of teaching English in isolation, CALLA uses English as a tool to learn subject matter. The objective of this model is to develop the academic language skills of learners with limited grammar accuracy (Steyn, 2017). CALLA integrates language development, explicit instruction and content area instruction in learning strategies. This approach relies strongly on scaffolding, i.e. the provision of instructional support with the first introduction of concepts and skills and the gradual removal of this support as learners develop greater proficiency, knowledge and skills of content introduced. CALLA can help Intermediate Phase learners in understanding and retaining content material while they are increasing their English language skills such as listening, speaking, reading and most importantly writing. The CALLA programme proposes a different order for introducing content-based instruction: firstly Science, secondly Mathematics and then Social Studies. The reasoning is that science entails the use of objects and equipment to illustrate concepts and principles and that working in co-operative groups will develop the language naturally. Mathematics content is assisted by the use of concrete objects and numeric symbols to decode the language. Social Studies require more literacy skills and are thus introduced last If CALLA should be implemented in the South African context, the order of introduction would have to be altered to Mathematics first, followed by Science and then Social Sciences. Because of difficulties experienced in teaching Mathematics to HL learners would acquire terminology more readily, as numerical symbols and concrete objects are used in Mathematics to decode language. Introducing science second would further support their English language development, as science also relies heavily on using concrete objects and practical experiments. Once the learners have internalised and embraced the language associated with Mathematics and Science, Social Sciences, which rely heavily on language, can be introduced. The Grade 3

Assessment Guide of the integrated Louisiana Educational Assessment Program follows the same order of Mathematics, Science and then Social Studies (Louisiana Department of Education, 2012).

Presentation-Practice-Production (Ppp) Model: According to Navaz & Sama (2017) the approach that is used in Sri Lanka for grammar teaching is the Presentation-Practice-Production (PPP) model. PPP is a method for teaching language structures in a foreign language. As its name suggests, PPP is divided into three phases, moving from tight teacher control towards greater learner freedom (Zohri, 2018). This model consists of a structured three-stage sequence for grammar instruction: a presentation stage, a practice stage, and a production stage. In the presentation stage, the new grammar rule or structure is introduced, usually through a text, a dialogue, or a story that includes the structure. In the practice stage, learners are given various kinds of written and spoken exercises to repeat or reproduce the new forms. Then the production stage comes, where learners are encouraged to use the rules that they have learned in the presentation and practice stages, more freely and in more communicative activities. The purpose of the presentation stage is to help learners become familiar with the new grammatical structure and keep it in their short-term memory, while the practice stage is to help learners gain control of the knowledge introduced in the presentation stage, and finally, the aim of the practice stage is to fully master the new form by enabling learners to internalize the rules and use them automatically and spontaneously, which helps develop fluency (Navaz & Sama, 2017).

Integration of Technoogical Tools in Language Teaching: The use of technology has become an important part of the learning process in and out of the class (Mohammad, 2018). Technology continues to grow in importance as a tool to help teachers facilitate language learning for their learners. The rise of technology integration has significantly contributed to the change in teaching writing in a second language. Using technology gives learners a safe venue for expressing their ideas without having to worry about handwriting or spelling mistakes. This method hones their vocabulary skills and gives them an opportunity to receive written feedback from an instructor, which in turn aids grammar accuracy. Ghandoura (2012) stresses that technology makes the acquisition of writing skills easier and faster. The benefit of this approach is that it gives an immediate alert to grammatical and spelling errors. In a rich technology, EFAL learners can become better in grammar (Ismail, Al-Awidi, & Almekhlafi, 2012). The researcher agrees with the above authors in terms of integrating the Fourth Industrial Revolution when teaching grammar because it makes it easier for the learner to learn through technology and it is also beneficial since the world keeps on changing. Websites and digital resources Websites and digital resources are a collection of public websites, personal websites and digital resources provided on the internet. Websites and digital resources have been recognized as important sources of linguistic and cultural knowledge for language learners to explore. EFAL learners can access the website through computers, mobile phones and other digital devices to get digital learning material. Lim (2018) explored the role of web portals in assisting learners in the search for and collection of vocabulary. The results indicated that, by using websites and digital resources, language learners performed vocabulary building tasks more effectively by searching for the required vocabulary and were able to build larger and richer vocabulary combinations as well as other grammar rules. The study also found that learners used websites with a specific focus rather than a general search engine (Lim, 2018). e-books A book which is composed in, or converted to, digital format for display on a computer screen or handheld device is an e-book (Chan, 2019). With the development of network technology, e-books as a teaching tool have been paid more and more attention in the language classroom. Teachers can compile language learning materials into e-books so that learners can have access to learning materials anytime and anywhere. Specific reading support cues, such as gloss and hypertext notes, have been embedded in e-books designed to promote language development (Chan, 2019). Robots Merriam-Webster Dictionary (2016) defines a robot as a machine that resembles a living creature. Robots are capable of moving and performing various actions. An anthropomorphic robot is considered as a useful educational tool because of its ability to improve teaching efficiency and learner motivation. It is found that robot-supported language learning is generally applied to younger learners. Wu, Wang and Chen (2015) carried out a study in which they investigated how teaching-assistant robots can help in primary schools. The robot is able to perform different forms of interaction with learners (e.g. gestures or facial expressions). Besides, physical activity was designed to engage and entertain learners, while enhancing grammar and their interest in learning through speaking and reacting. Human-like or cartoon-like external appearances of robots play an important role when used for young learners. A familiar, interesting appearance is effective to learners who have poor language proficiency, particularly in grammar when writing or afraid to speak in English in front of peers. Advantages of using technology to enhance grammar in learners doing EFAL Technology is an effective tool for learners. It increases learners' cooperation. Technology helps teachers meet their learners' educational needs. According to Mohammad (2018), technology enables teachers and learners to make local and global societies connect with the people thereby expanding opportunities for their learning. The application of technology has considerably changed English grammar teaching methods. It provides so many alternatives and as making teaching interesting and more productive in terms of advancement (Patel, 2013). In traditional classrooms, teachers stand in front of learners and give lectures, explanations, and instructions through using the blackboard or whiteboard. These method must be changed to include the development of technology. Technology encourages learners to learn individually and to acquire responsible behaviours. The independent use of technologies gives learners self-direction. According to Arifah (2014), the use of the internet increases learners' motivation. It helps learners to realize the topic with enthusiasm and develop their knowledge; it also assists learners in developing their higher order thinking skills. It can be concluded that the true integration of technology is very important to attract learners' attention towards English grammar learning.

Research Methodology: The paper is channeled by an overarching question: what are the preeminent practices that can be employed to enrich English proficiency in Efal learners? This paper adopted a qualitative research method based on interpretive paradigm and followed a case study as a research design. In this study, the researcher intended to unearth the determinants in the indecent use of syntax in Efal learners. According to (Moodley, 2013), qualitative research, which is a study of phenomena in their natural settings, attempts to make sense of, or to interpret phenomena in terms of the meanings people attach to them. The target population comprised of 4 educators and 6 learners from one primary school located in Umfolozi circuit in the province of KwaZulu-Natal under King Cetshwayo District, Richards Bay area was selected purposively. Both teachers and learners varied in gender, age, and experience in the field of education. Participants were selected subject to their availability and willingness to take part in the study as well as meeting the requirement of the study. The researcher's judgment was used to choose teachers who were knowledgeable of the subject matter, who have been in the field for more than five years and those who were considered to be information-rich. In terms of selecting learners, the researcher selected learners aged between 10 to 11 years in Grade 5 doing EFAL. The study consisted of ten (10) participants who were interviewed (4 educators as well as 6 leaners); six interviewees were recorded as 4 participants did not consent to being recorded. Interviews were transcribed and analyzed using thematic analysis. The participants in the study consisted of both male and female educators aged 30 to 55 as well as male and female learners aged 10 to11. The reason for selecting 4 educators is that the study will focus on 1 selected primary school; usually there are a few educators teaching that particular grade, so it will be difficult to equate number of teachers with a number of learners.

Results And Discussion

The findings presented herein provide evidence that current methods are simply not moving EFAL learners to the level of proficiency that is expected of them. It also appears that teachers rely solely on traditional methods. To assists learners with limited English proficiency it is recommended that teachers make content comprehensible through the use of different pedagogies drawn from research to enrich proficiency and to ensure that these learners master content with success. The literature further reveals that teachers are reluctant to integrate technology during language teaching thus because they think it's time consuming, some have technophobia. Many lack the knowledge on how to integrate ICT or technology into the curriculum.

Conclusion: This paper has reached the conclusion that for proficiency to be enriched, new methods should be introduced and for enhancement to be effective, technology should be integrated into the curriculum. It is without a doubt that the application of best methodologies will lay a solid foundation for successful academic performance in the future. Learners will master the content with success. Apart from this, being exposed to technology will make EFAL learners develop their verbal and non- verbal communication skills in and outside the classroom. Their fluency and proficiency in language will even provide them the opportunity to access higher education and enter the labour market with confidence.

References

1. Al Hosni, R. Z. S. (2019). Professional Development (PD) at the Colleges of Technology in Oman: An Inquiry into English Language Centres' Staff Perceptions of their PD, PD Needs, Current PD Provision and PD Enhancement. University of Exeter (United Kingdom).

2. Al-Mekhlafi, A. M. & Nagaratnam, R. P. (2011). Difficulties in Teaching and Learning Grammar in an EFL Context. International Journal of Instruction, 4(2), 69-92.and strategies." British Journal of Social Sciences, 76-93Arabia. Educational Research, 2(7), 1248-1257.

3. Department of Basic Education. 2015. Annual National Assessment 2014: Diagnostic Report - First Additional Language and Home Language. Retrieved from: http://www.education.gov.za

4. Ghandoura, W. A. (2012). A Qualitative Study of ESL College Students' Attitudes about Computer-Assisted Writing Classes. English language teaching, 5(4), 57-64.

5. Lim, C. P., Tinio, V. L., Smith, M., & Bhowmik, M. K. (2018). Digital learning for developing Asian countries: Achieving equity, quality, and efficiency in education. Routledge international handbook of schools and schooling in Asia, 369-381.

6. Mohammad, T., & Hazarika, Z. (2016). Difficulties of learning EFL in KSA: Writing skills in context. International Journal of English Linguistics, 6(3), 105-117.

7. Moodley, V. (2013). In-service teacher education: Asking questions for higher order thinking in visual literacy. South African Journal of Education, 33(2).

8. Navaz, A. M. M., & Sama, F. R. F. (2017). Teaching grammar in the English language classroom: perceptions and practices of students and teachers in the Ampara district.

9. Odden, D. (2013). Introducing phonology. Cambridge University Press.

10. Patel, J. (2013). Effectiveness of Language Games to Enhance Spoken Competence of ESL of Class VIII Students (Doctoral dissertation, Waymade College of Education).

11. Patel, J. (2013). Effectiveness of Language Games to Enhance Spoken Competence of ESL of Class VIII Students (Doctoral dissertation, Waymade College of Education).

12.Patton, M. Q. (2007). Sampling, qualitative (purposive). The Blackwell Encyclopaedia of Sociology.

13.Schmid, H. J. (2012). Linguistic theories, approaches, and methods. In English and American studies: Theory and practice (pp. 371-394). Stuttgart: JB Metzler.

14.Steyn, G. (2017). The transition of Grade 4 learners to English as medium of instruction (Doctoral dissertation, University of Pretoria).

15.Taylor, S. & von Fintel, M. 2016. Estimating the impact of language of instruction in South African primary schools: A fixed effects approach. Economics of Education Review, 50:75-89.

16.Wu, W. C. V., Wang, R. J., & Chen, N. S. (2015). Instructional design using an in-house built teaching assistant robot to enhance elementary school English-as-a-foreign-language learning. Interactive Learning Environments, 23(6), 696-714.

17.Zhou, P., Crain, S., & Zhan, L. (2014). Grammatical aspect and event recognition in children's online sentence comprehension. Cognition, 133(1), 262-276.

8. Muscle Head: Online Gym Management System.

Salvador Consultado Jr, Juan Angelo Fraginal, Francis Eli Vargas, John Russell Viaña, Roberto Acepcion Jr and Rhonnel Paculanan

Arellano University, **Philippines**

Introduction

Gym activities have gone digital. A gym website makes it simple and convenient for consumers to use gym services from their homes or wherever else they can access the internet. It is not necessary to physically enter the gym in order to gather information about the fitness programs, classes, and other services that are offered. People are able to explore numerous features and conduct information searches on each program by browsing the website, allowing them to make knowledgeable decisions with only a few clicks. [1] One of the helpful tools offered by a gym website is a selection of training videos, exercise manuals, and fitness consultations. These services cater to consumers of all fitness levels and offer advices on various exercises and techniques. Users can access a library of exercise videos to view on their own in order to guarantee proper technique and maximize performance. Additionally, there are in the websites, fitness suggestions

that offer guidance on healthy eating and general wellbeing. [2] In order to make exercises easier for users, a gym website offers convenience, access, and a wealth of resources. Users are able to customize their training routine, train properly and acquire knowledge on nutrition and overall well-being through browsing fitness programs and educational programs, with access to workout videos, exercise guides or exercise tips. In addition, users also benefit from the inclusion of a food planner feature that enables them to maintain an optimal diet. [3] Due to an increased awareness of the importance of healthy lifestyles, the fitness industry has seen strong growth and transformation. Active efforts are being made by humans to increase their fitness levels. Nevertheless, the limitations of traditional gym models include geographic restrictions, reduced working hours and crowded facilities. These factors can make it more difficult for people to access the services of a gymnasium, and achieve their fitness objectives in an effective way. [4] Online platforms that provide comfort, accessibility, and flexibility have revolutionized the fitness business thanks to digital technologies. Since the internet plays such a significant role in people's lives, online gym systems give people the chance to reach a larger audience, provide individualized services, and get beyond the constraints of conventional gym rooms. [5] Benefits such as remote access to fitness information, class dates, and progress monitoring are provided by the deployment of an online gym website system. In addition, the company offers personal trainers, nutrition guidance, and tools for tracking health indicators. Leveraging technology improves the user experience, stimulates engagement, and creates a personal approach to exercising without the constraints of conventional gym rooms. [6] The aim of the online gym management system serves as a solution to users fitness needs allowing people to work out anywhere as long as they have internet access. It will provides the following benefits (1) Access to a library of workout video tutorials. It categorizes different types of classes such as strength training. Members choose the videos they want to follow or try. (2) Offer an online scheduling system where users can schedule their virtual workout sessions based on available time slots. It also includes a reminder system to notify members about their scheduled workout sessions and other related notices. (3) Provide digital calculator to compute user's body mass index (BMI). Users have to input their height and weight. The system then calculates their BMI and provides an interpretation of the result. (4) To access a food planner that the users need to follow for their calorie intake to achieve their body goals.

Methodology

The research design employed is quantitative method to investigate the effectiveness of an online gym website. The study collected data on user's engagements and satisfaction through the website and quantified it. The findings provided insights into the impact of website features on user engagements and satisfaction, and improvements to enhance the overall user experience of the online gym platform. The Software Development Life Cycle (SDLC) is a methodology that partitions the development tasks into portions instead of trying to develop the application in general at the same time. Each part goes through stages, like analysis of requirements, planning, designing, coding, testing, review, and launching. Agile Methodology will be the SDLC.

Figure 1. Agile Methodology

Database plan alludes to a bunch of tasks that work with the creation, improvement, execution, and upkeep of a database framework for an organization. By planning a data set appropriately, the cost of support can be decreased, which thusly further develops data consistency and cost-effective measures, especially as far as disk storage space. Thusly, designers must carry out viable and productive ideas, and stick to rules while guaranteeing that all components of the database are interrelated.

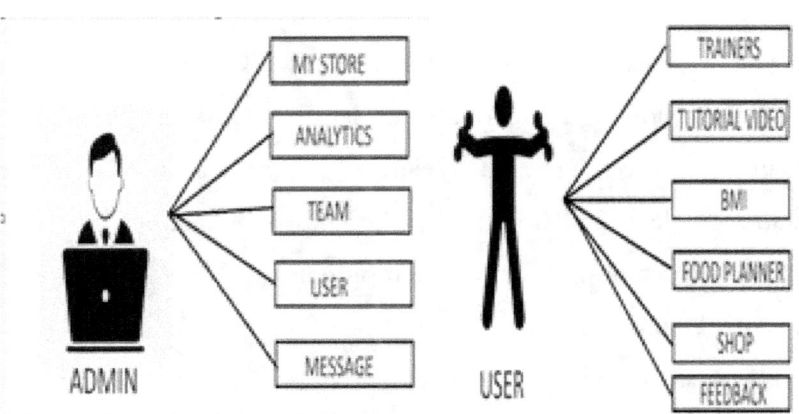

Figure 2: Use Case Diagram.

The figure above shows the Use Case Diagram. The User represents the person who usually the one to navigate the website while the admin refers to the system administrator. The features component includes the various functionalities accessible to the user, such as tutorial video, BMI, Food Planner, shop and Feedback. The system administration's panel components represent the administrative interface accessible only to the system administration, providing complete control over all aspects of the website.

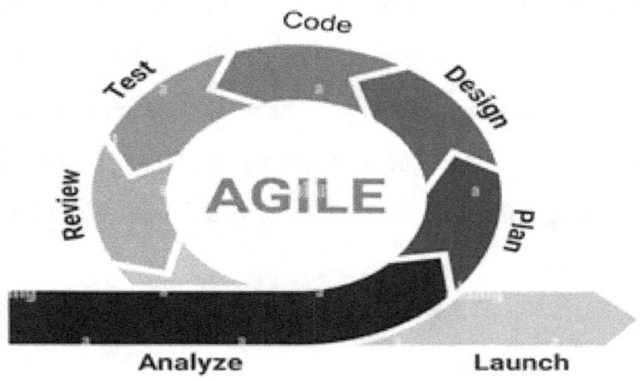

The project was tested by software criteria of ISO 25010 evaluation form with the following Functionality, Reliability, Efficiency, Usability, and Security. Percentage and Weighted Means was used for the computation of ISO 25010 and with the help of Likert Scale for the range and Interpretation of the data computed.

Results And Discussion

Muscle Head, an online gym management system designed to cater to individuals' fitness requirements. It offers a web-based platform allowing users to exercise from anywhere with internet access. This online gym management system aims to assist people in enhancing their physical strength or adopting a healthier lifestyle, eliminating the need to commute to a traditional gym for workouts. The system is constructed utilizing development tools that include HTML, PHP, CSS, and JavaScript. Shows the comparison of evaluations of User and Technical-Respondents. Male users' overall average mean is 3.8 interpreted as "Highly Satisfied" while male technical respondents' overall average mean is 3.8 interpreted as "Highly Satisfied". Female users' overall average mean is 3.7 interpreted as "Highly Satisfied" while female technical respondents' overall average mean is 3.8 interpreted as "Highly Satisfied. All respondents (users and technical) are highly satisfied on the acceptability and usage of the application.

Summary of Findings

Gym Management System holds a significant importance to people without a gym equipment or close to a gym facility. The System is best when it comes to Facilitating Fitness Goals, Safety and Maintenance, Variety of Service, Support and Guidance, Accountability and Consistency and Overall well-being of the system. Gym Management System is a web-based platform any software that has access to an network connection through the internet rather than being stored in a device's memory. Web based application will run within the web browser. Likewise, ISO 25010 evaluation format is used by users and technical respondents in the evaluation of the acceptability and usability of the application. This study is significant to gym management system owners and users of the system. Over-all this system has a user-friendly interface.

Conclusion: The study is able to identify the genders of the respondents as male and female. The evaluation's findings indicate that both male and female users, IT, CS, gym users, and technical responders strongly agree with the system. According to the findings, more male and female users than technical responders participated in this evaluation.

Recommendations

It is advised by the researchers to create a system that you are able to operate on. Know your strengths and weaknesses and rely on your own abilities. We recommend that in order to improve the project, researchers in the future get feedback from users so they can identify which features need improvement.

References

[1] Gym Management System (2019) St. Xavier's College, Maitighar https://www.coursehero.com/file/41259401/Introduction-of-the-Gym-Management-Systepdf/

[2] Gym Management System (2016) studylib https://studylib.net/doc/9571026/synopsis-project-title--gym-management-system-introduction

[3] Gym Website (2017) freeprojectz https://www.freeprojectz.com/project-report/6128

[4] GYM Management System (2019) PULAGAM MEENA SURYA KUMARIDept of CS ,SVKP & Dr K S Raju Arts & Science College, Penugond a, A.P, India,

https://thinkindiaquarterly.org/index.php/think-india/article/view/19499/14372

[5] Web based Gym Management System (2017) A dissertation submitted for the Degree of Master of Information Technology K G S T Gamage University of Colombo School of Computing https://dl.ucsc.cmb.ac.lk/jspui/bitstream/123456789/3899/1/2012MIT012.pdf

[6] Gym Management System P4P 2 (2019) LYCEUM OF THE PHILIPPINES - LAGUNA Km. 54 National Highway, Makiling, Calamba City, Laguna - Leyva, Melvin https://www.scribd.com/document/409083890/Gym-Management-System-P4P-2-docx

[7] Gym management software system (2019) - Firebug Software http://www.firebugsoftware.com/

[8] Smart Gym Management System (2020) A.V. Dinesh Kumar, K Bhargav Ram Rayal, M.Saraswathi International Journal of Scientific Research & Engineering Trends Volume 6 https://www.scribd.com/document/552614841/Ijsret-v6-Issue3-493

[9] Gym Management Information System (2015) Landrito, Jericho https://prezi.com/5ozvuwlxdz5y/gym-management/

[10] Implementing a Web Based Client Information System in FV Fitness Gym in El Salvador City, Misamis Oriental (2021) - A Bachelor's Thesis Presented to the Faculty of College in Business and

Technology, Saint Paul University Quezon City - De Leon April Marie T and Tinsay, Andrea Mae B

9. Issues and Challenges: A Study of the Indian Banking Sector.

Poonam[1] and Dr. Savita Choudhary[2]

[1]Research Scholar, Department of Management Studies, Swami Keshvanand Institute of Technology, Management & Gramothan, Rajasthan Technical University, Kota, RJ, **India**

[2]Associate Professor, Department of Management Studies, Swami Keshvanand Institute of Technology, Management & Gramothan, Rajasthan Technical University, Kota, RJ, **India**

Abstract: The Indian banking sector faces diverse challenges including regulatory changes, technological advancements, and addressing the needs of a diverse customer base. However, these challenges also present opportunities for growth and development. Reforms have been essential for the sector's adaptation to changing economic landscapes. Technological advancements have improved efficiency and customer service, but require continuous upskilling and cybersecurity measures. Regulatory challenges impact various banking operations, necessitating careful navigation. Banks must cater to the rising demand for diverse services while ensuring profitability. Growth opportunities include the country's favorable demographic trends and initiatives for financial inclusion and digital literacy. Overall, embracing innovation and adapting to changing dynamics is crucial for the Indian banking sector to thrive. The objective of this paper is to explain the changing banking scenario, to study the challenges and opportunities of Indian banks, and to analyze the impact. In conclusion, while the Indian banking sector faces various challenges, it also holds immense potential for innovation and growth. By embracing technological advancements, navigating regulatory changes, and catering to evolving customer needs, Indian banks can overcome these challenges and thrive in today's dynamic business environment.

Keywords: Issues and Challenges, Banking sector and Reform.

Introduction: We have seen recently that the global economy is going through some complex situations, such as the crisis in the eurozone, the bankruptcy of banks and financial institutions, and the global debt crisis. Major economies including the US and Europe are experiencing a recession as a result of the increasingly unstable situation. This raises several important concerns regarding the continuation, expansion, and sustainability of development. Nevertheless, India's banking sector has been one of the few to remain resilient in the face of all this chaos. Over the last ten years, the Indian banking sector has developed at an astounding rate. The fact that Indian banking is strong and vigorous is obvious from the faster rate of loan expansion, rising profitability and productivity that are comparable to those of banks in developed economies, the decreased frequency of non-performing assets, and the emphasis on financial inclusion. The banking industry in India is confronted with a multitude of obstacles, such as modifications to regulations, progress in technology, and meeting the requirements of a varied clientele. These difficulties do, yet, also offer chances for improvement and progress. To maintain the momentum of the economy, Indian banks have started to reassess the opportunities available and adjust their growth strategy. A conscious effort has been made to review the several issues that the Indian banking industry is anticipated to confront in this paper.

Objectives of the Study: The main objective of this paper is to explain the changing banking scenario and to study the challenges of Indian banks.

Conceptual Clarification: Historical Background

The foundation of modern banking in India traces back to the establishment of the Bank of Hindustan in 1870, followed by the Presidential Bank Act of 1876, which created three presidential banks: the Bank of Calcutta, the Bank of Bombay, and the Bank of Madras. These banks laid the groundwork for the Imperial Bank of India, formed in 1921 by amalgamating the presidential banks. Before the establishment of the Reserve Bank of India (RBI) in 1934, the Imperial Bank performed limited central banking functions alongside its commercial banking operations, except for foreign exchange dealings. The RBI Act of 1934 marked the formal establishment of the RBI as the apex banking institution, initially with significant non-government ownership. Subsequently, the Banking Regulations Act of 1949 further regulated the banking sector, solidifying the framework for modern banking in India. The Reserve Bank of India (RBI) came under governmental oversight with the enactment of a statute granting it broad authority to regulate banks, issue licenses, and conduct inspections. In 1955, the RBI took over the Imperial Bank of India, renaming it the State Bank of India (SBI). Subsequently, in 1959, SBI absorbed eight private banks, making them its subsidiaries. By 1960, the RBI gained the power to enforce mergers between weak and strong banks, leading to a significant reduction in the number of banks by 1969. The government then nationalized 14 banks in 1969 and six more in 1980 to foster economic growth. Following the Narasimha Committee report in 1992, which recommended extensive reforms, new private-sector banks emerged after amendments to the Banking Regulation Act in 1993. Despite global economic crises, India's banking laws and regulatory structure have shielded it from severe impacts. Understanding the Indian banking sector's structure and context is crucial to navigating its opportunities and challenges amidst global economic uncertainties.

Indian Banking Sector: The Indian banking sector operates within the regulatory framework overseen by the Reserve Bank of India (RBI), serving as the central bank. This sector primarily comprises Commercial Banks and Co-operative Banks. Within the commercial banking structure, we have Scheduled Commercial Banks, which are those listed in the Second Schedule of the RBI Act, 1934, meeting specific criteria set by the RBI. This status offers benefits like access to RBI accommodations during liquidity constraints but also entails compliance with reserve regulations. Co-operative banks, though not all are included in the Second Schedule, also play a significant role. To assess performance, the RBI categorizes banks into Public Sector Banks, Old Private Sector Banks, New Private Sector Banks, and Foreign Banks. Additionally, other entities such as Regional Rural Banks, Urban Cooperative Banks, and Rural Cooperative Credit Institutions contribute to the diversity of the banking landscape in India

Reserve Bank of India (Regulatory Authority)

1. Bank

    a.Scheduled Commercial Banks

        •Public Sector Banks

        •Private Sector Banks (Old & New)

        •Foreign Banks

    b.Co-operative Credit Institutions

        •Regional Rural Banks

        •Urban Cooperative Banks

        •Rural Cooperative Credit Institutions

2. Financial Institution

    a.All India Financial Institution

    b.State-Level Institution

    c.Other Institution

Issues and Challenges: For Indian Banks, the current environment has brought up several opportunities as well as challenges. Understanding the opportunities and difficulties facing the Indian banking sector is necessary to comprehend the overall state of the industry. **Rural Market:** India's banking industry is typically rather developed in terms of supply, product selection, and reach, while access to rural areas is still a barrier for foreign and private banks operating there. Compared to other banks in similar economies in the region, Indian banks are thought to have clean, strong, and transparent balance sheets in terms of capital adequacy and asset quality As a result, to meet impending problems in the Indian banking industry, some nationalized and private sector banks have followed some examples of inorganic growth strategies. For instance, ICICI Bank Ltd. recently merged with the Bank of Rajasthan Ltd. to greatly expand its market share and reach in rural areas. State Bank of India (SBI), the largest public sector bank in India has also adopted the same strategy to retain its position. It is in the process of acquiring its associates. Recently, SBI has merged State Bank of Indore in 2010.

Management of Risks: The level of rivalry among banks is rising as a result of this. However, the current state of the global banking landscape poses significant risks to the Indian banking sector. Some overseas banks have already declared bankruptcy. According to Shrieves (1992), increases in capital are positively correlated with risk increases. The findings of the study, which examined a sizable sample of banks, show that regulation was only partially successful over the researched time. Furthermore, it was determined that variations in bank capital during the examined period were contingent on risk.

Sensarma and Jayadev (2009) employed a few chosen accounting measures as risk management factors to evaluate banks' general risk management capacity. They summarized these accounting ratios using multivariate statistical methods. Additionally, regression analysis was used in the paper to examine how these risk management ratings affected stock returns. Researchers discovered that over time, Indian banks have become more adept at managing risk. The ability of banks to manage risk seemed to have an impact on stock returns. According to the report, banks that wish to increase shareholder wealth should concentrate on effectively managing a variety of risks.

Growth of Banking: Zhao, Casu, and Ferrari (2008) employed a Malmquist Total Factor Productivity (TFP) index based on Data Envelopment Analysis (DEA) and a balanced panel data set spanning the years 1992–2004. The empirical analysis showed that, mostly due to technological advancement, the Indian banking sector had consistent productivity growth following an initial period of adjustment. The ownership structure of banks does not appear to be as important as more competition in terms of TFP growth. When competition grew, foreign banks seemed to take the lead in technical innovation, which heightened the pressure on the banking industry to compete. Lastly, our findings also suggest that the deregulation process as a whole is leading to an increase in risk-taking behavior. It was found in the study of Goyal and Joshi (2011a) Due to their inability to handle the effects of the global economy, small and local banks require assistance, which is one of the driving forces behind mergers. Mergers were employed by certain private banks as a calculated tactic to broaden their reach. India's rural markets have enormous potential that the big banks haven't yet looked into. As a result, mergers have been ICICI Bank Ltd.'s method of market expansion in rural areas. Their attempt to establish themselves in rural India is successful. It increases their market share, customer base, and network strength beyond geographic boundaries.**Market Discipline and Transparency:** According to Fernando (2011) In the new environment, standards for transparency and disclosure as components of globally recognized corporate governance procedures are becoming more significant. It is expected of banks to be more accountable and responsive to investors. Banks are required to include a plethora of information in their balance sheets, including the maturity profiles of their assets and liabilities, lending to sensitive industries, changes in non-performing assets (NPAs), capital, provisions, government shareholdings, the value of their investments in India and overseas, operational and profitability indicators, the total amount invested in equity shares, mutual fund units, bonds, debentures, aggregate advances against shares, and so forth. **Human Resource Management:** Gelade and Ivery (2003) investigated the connections between organizational performance, work environment, and human resource management (HRM) in a retail bank's branch network. There are strong relationships between corporate performance, HR procedures, and work environment. The findings supported a mediation model in which work climate acts as a partial mediating factor between the impacts of HRM practices on business performance, and they demonstrated that the correlations between climate and performance could not be explained by their shared reliance on HRM elements. **Global Banking:** Any country cannot conceivably and fundamentally exclude itself from the global economy. Thus, integration processes such as globalization and liberalization must be adopted for sustainable growth, just as India opened its doors to foreign businesses in 1991. Due to their inevitable competition with multinational businesses, domestic businesses face difficulties as a result of globalization. 36 foreign banks are operating in India, which presents a significant threat to nationalized and private sector banks, according to an analysis of the country's banking sector. Due to their scale, technological sophistication, and global market presence, these foreign banks provide Indian traders with a greater range of options and services. **Financial Inclusion:** Dev (2006) declared that the living conditions of the impoverished, farmers, rural non-farm businesses, and other disadvantaged populations make financial inclusion important. Financial inclusion refers to the ability of different social groups to obtain loans from official institutions. The author concludes that, in addition to traditional banking institutions, which ought to view inclusion as a social obligation as well as an economic opportunity, the self-help group movement and microfinance institutions play a significant role in enhancing financial inclusion. According to the research, this calls for new regulatory processes and the financial sector to be depoliticized. **Employees' Retention:** Over the past ten years, the banking sector has seen a tremendous transformation. It went from being transactional and focused on providing customer service to becoming more competitive and prioritizing revenue growth. Experienced bank workers are growing disillusioned with the sector and frequently refuse to meet the higher standards. Revenue declines as a result of declining staff morale. Owing to the inherently intimate bonds that exist between employees and clients, removing those personnel entirely may result in the loss of important client connections. Because competitors are always coming in to hire them away, the retail banking sector is worried about staff retention at all levels, from tellers to executives to customer service personnel. There is a fierce rivalry to keep important staff. Top-level executives and HR departments spend large amounts of time, effort, and money trying to figure out how to keep their people from leaving Sekaran, U. (1989) This study, which included a sample of 267 bank workers, followed the pathways leading from job participation and sense of competence—two quality of life factors—to employees' job satisfaction at work. The findings showed that factors related to people's personal, professional, and organizational climates affected their ego investment or job involvement, which in turn affected the intra-psychic reward of feeling competent that they experienced, which in turn affected workers' job satisfaction

Customer Retention: Levesque and McDougall (1996) examined the key factors that affect consumer satisfaction and ambitions for the future in the retail banking industry. Service quality dimensions (e.g., doing it correctly the first time), service features (e.g., competitive interest rates), service difficulties, service recovery, and items used are some of the determinants that they discovered. It was discovered, specifically, that customer happiness and intent to switch are significantly impacted by service issues and the bank's capacity to recover from them. Clark (1997) investigated how a large UK retail bank's client retention rates were affected by employee-customer interactions. He disclosed that there exists a relationship between employee and customer perceptions of service quality and customer retention rates, as well as a relationship between employee and consumer perceptions of service quality. **Environmental Concerns:** The newly established Copenhagen Climate Council (CCC) makes it abundantly evident that all nations in the globe urgently need to raise public awareness of environmental issues. The Thought Leadership Series on Climate Change, produced by CCC, is an anthology of thought-provoking, succinct, and persuasive essays on climate change written by some of the most well-known intellectuals and business leaders in the world. The articles aim to communicate the message that action is needed and to help increase public and political understanding of the activities that could have a major impact on the growth of global emissions. The goal of the Thought Leadership Series was to elucidate and disseminate the essential components of the business and policy response to the climate crisis. The rationale for the Thought Leadership Series was to change the focus of people. **Social and Ethical Aspects:** Certain banks take it upon themselves to actively assume the social and ethical responsibilities associated with banking. It presents a challenge to commercial banks to take these factors into account in their activities. Commercial banks are expected to fund organizations that address social issues in addition to maximizing profits. Benedikter (2011) defines Social Banks as "banks with a conscience". Their main priorities include community investment, opportunity provision for the underprivileged, and advocacy for social, environmental, and ethical causes. Social banks make an effort to solely allocate their funds to projects that advance the common good rather than ones that benefit a select few privately. Additionally, he has outlined the primary distinction between mainstream and social banks, emphasizing that the former typically use the triple concept of profit—people, planet, and profit—while the latter focuses only on maximizing of profits

Research Methodology: The research methodology will encompass a comprehensive approach, combining quantitative and qualitative methods to address the complex challenges and opportunities within the Indian banking sector. Quantitative analysis will involve gathering financial data from diverse sources and applying statistical techniques such as regression analysis to examine factors like capital adequacy and risk management. Comparative analysis will assess the performance of different bank categories. Qualitative methods will include literature reviews, case studies of successful banks, and interviews/surveys with industry experts to gain nuanced insights into emerging trends and strategies. Through triangulation and synthesis of findings, the research aims to provide actionable recommendations for policymakers and banking institutions, facilitating sustainable growth and development. An iterative process will ensure depth and rigor in the research, enhancing the understanding of the sector as a whole.

Conclusion:

Over time, it has been noted that two significant market phenomena—clouds of dread and dips of growth—frequently fluctuate depending on the circumstances. Numerous environmental changes that have occurred both before and after liberalization have had a direct impact on the aforementioned phenomena. It is clear that India has seen tremendous growth in the post-liberalization era, but there have also been some difficulties. Several opportunities and problems are covered in this article, including the rural market, transparency, consumer expectations, risk management, banking sector expansion, the human aspect, global banking, environmental concerns, social and ethical issues, and staff and customer retention. Banks are working hard to stay ahead of the competition. The competition from global banks and technological innovation has compelled the banks to rethink their policies and strategies.

References:

[1] Shrieves, R. E. "The relationship between risk and capital in commercial banks". Journal of Banking & Finance, 16(2): 439–457, 1992.

[2] Wolgast, M. "M&As in the financial industry: A matter of concern for bank supervisors?" Journal of Financial Regulation and Compliance, 9(3): 225-236, 2001.

[3] Al-Tamimi, H. A. H and Al-Mazrooei, F. M. "Banks' risk management: A comparison study of UAE national and foreign banks". Journal of Risk Finance, 8(4): 394-409, 2007.

[4] Sensarma, R. and Jayadev, "Are bank stocks sensitive to risk management?" Journal of Risk Finance, 10(1): 7-22, M. 2009.

[5] Zhao, T., Casu, B. and Ferrari, A. "Deregulation and Productivity Growth: A Study of The Indian Commercial Banking Industry". International Journal of Business Performance Management, 10(4): 318-343, 2008.

[6] Goyal, K. A. and Joshi, V. "Mergers in Banking Industry of India: Some Emerging Issues". Asian Journal of Business and Management Sciences, 1(2): 157-165, 2011a.

[7] Fernando, A. C. "Business Environment". Noida: Dorling Kindersley (India) Pvt. Ltd. (2011), pp. 549-553.

[8] Gelade, G. A. and Ivery, M. "The Impact of Human Resource Management and Work Climate on Organizational Performance". Personnel Psychology, 56(2): 383-404, 2003.

[9] Bartel, A. P. "Human Resource Management and Organizational Performance: Evidence from Retail Banking". Industrial and Labor Relations Review, 57(2): 181-203, 2004.

[10] Dev, S. M. "Financial Inclusion: Issues and Challenges". Economic & Political Weekly, 41(41): 2006.

[11] Sekaran, U. "Paths to the job satisfaction of bank employees". Journal of Organizational Behavior, 10(4): 347-359, 1989.

[12] Mitchell, T R., Holtom, B. C., Lee, T. W. and Graske, T. "How to Keep Your Best Employees: Developing an Effective Retention Policy". The Academy of Management Executive, 15(4): 96-109, 2001.

[13] Saxena, N. and Monika, K. "Organizational Culture and its Impact on Employee Retention". Pacific Business Review, 2(3): 102-110, 2010.

[14] Levesque, T. and McDougall, G.H.G. "Determinants of Customer Satisfaction in Retail Banking". International Journal of Bank Marketing, 14(7): 12 – 20, 1996.

[15] Clark, M. "Modelling the Impact of Customer-Employee Relationships on Customer Retention Rates in a Major UK Retail Bank". Management Decision, 35(4): 293-301, 1997.

[16] Clark, M. "The Relationship between Employees' Perceptions of Organizational Climate and Customer Retention Rates in a Major UK Retail Bank". Journal of Strategic Marketing, 10(2): 93-113, 2002.

[17] Hansemark, O. C. and Albinsson, M. "Customer Satisfaction and Retention: The Experiences of Individual Employees". Managing Service Quality, 14(1): 40 – 57, 2004.

[18] Benedikter, R. "Answers to the Economic Crisis: Social Banking and Social Finance". Spice Digest, New York: Springer. (2011).

[19] Goyal, K. A. and Joshi, V. "A Study of Social and Ethical Issues in Banking Industry". International Journal of Economics & Research, 2011 2(5): 49-57, 2011b.

10. Cloud Economics: Unlocking Business Value for Digital NBFC Businesses.

Dnyaneshwar Raosaheb Gaikwad

Bharati Vidyapeeth Deemed University IMRDA ,Sangli , Maharashtra, **India**

Abstract: In the dynamic landscape of the Indian financial sector, Non-Banking Financial Companies (NBFCs) are embracing digitalization to thrive. This document explores how Cloud Economics, the study of managing and optimizing cloud computing costs, empowers digital NBFCs to unlock significant business value across various aspects, including product, price, promotion, and place.

Keywords :- Cloud , Cloud Economics, Cloud cost efficiency

Introoduction

History of the Term "Cloud Economics" While the exact origin of the term "Cloud Economics" remains unclear, its emergence coincides with the rapid adoption of cloud computing in the late 2000s and early 2010s. As businesses started migrating their workloads to the cloud, a need arose to understand and manage the associated financial implications. Here's a possible timeline of the term's evolution: Pre-2008: Cloud computing is still in its infancy, and the focus is on technical aspects rather than financial considerations. 2008-2010: Cloud adoption grows rapidly, raising concerns about cost management and the need for financial accountability. Early mentions of terms like "cloud cost management" and "cloud financial management" begin to appear. 2011-2013: The term "Cloud Economics" gains wider recognition as businesses seek solutions to optimize their cloud investments. Industry conferences and publications start addressing cloud economics, and research studies explore its principles and practices. 2014-2016: Cloud service providers (CSPs) like AWS, Azure, and Google Cloud introduce dedicated tools and services for cloud cost management and financial optimization. The FinOps Foundation is established to promote best practices for cloud financial management. Cloud Economics becomes a standard practice for businesses leveraging cloud computing, with specialized roles and expertise emerging. Research and development in the field continue, leading to advancements in cloud cost optimization tools and methodologies. Present and Future: Cloud Economics continues to evolve as cloud technologies and business models become increasingly complex. The focus shifts from simply reducing costs to optimizing cloud investments for maximum business value. Cloud Economics expands to include broader aspects like sustainability and environmental impact of cloud usage. Key Contributors to the

Development of Cloud Economics: Cloud Service Providers (CSPs): AWS, Azure, Google Cloud, and others play a major role in developing cloud cost management tools and promoting Cloud Economics practices. FinOps Foundation: This non-profit organization establishes best practices and promotes the adoption of Cloud Economics principles. Industry Experts and Consultants: Consultants and advisors specialize in cloud cost optimization and provide guidance to businesses. Academic Research: Research institutions and universities contribute to the field through studies and publications on Cloud Economics.

The Power of Cloud Economics:

Cloud Economics equips NBFCs with the tools and strategies to: Optimize Costs: Pay-as-you-go models eliminate upfront infrastructure investments, and Cloud Economics practices further minimize waste and reduce costs. Scale with Agility: Respond rapidly to market fluctuations and customer demands by scaling cloud resources up or down as needed. Enhance Security and Compliance: Robust cloud security features and compliance certifications ensure data safety and adherence to regulatory requirements. Improve Customer Experience: Deliver a seamless and personalized experience through convenient online access and faster processing times. Fuel Innovation: Leverage cloud analytics to gain insights into customer behaviour and market trends, enabling the development of data-driven offerings. Cloud Economics and Business Values: Cloud Economics influences digital NBFC business values at both micro and macro levels: Micro Level: Reduced operational costs: Streamlined processes and optimized resource usage lead to cost savings. Increased agility: Rapid scaling and deployment of new services improve responsiveness to market shifts and customer needs. Enhanced customer satisfaction: Improved online experience and faster service delivery lead to happier customers. Data-driven decision making: Cloud analytics provide valuable insights for informed business decisions. Macro Level: Sustainable growth: Cost optimization and agility contribute to long-term financial stability and growth. Enhanced market reach: Cloud-based platforms enable NBFCs to expand their reach beyond geographical limitations. Increased competitiveness: Improved efficiency and innovation provide a competitive edge in the market. Contribution to financial inclusion: Digital NBFCs can reach underserved populations with accessible financial services. Cloud Economics Impact on Product, Price, Promotion, and Place on NBFC's in India : **Product:** Cloud-based platforms allow NBFCs to offer personalized products, such as tailored loan options based on customer profiles. NBFCs can experiment and iterate on new products more readily due to the agility of cloud infrastructure. Example: A large NBFC's in India developed a cloud-based loan processing system, reducing processing time by 20% and enabling faster loan approvals. Price: Dynamic pricing models based on usage can be implemented, offering more cost-effective solutions for specific customer segments. Cloud-based analytics provide insights into customer price sensitivity, enabling NBFCs to optimize pricing strategies. Example: A Bank backed NBFC in India transitioned to the cloud and reduced IT infrastructure costs by 30%, allowing them to offer more competitive product pricing. Promotion: Cloud-based marketing platforms provide extensive data and analytics, enabling NBFCs to personalize their communication and campaigns for better engagement. Social media and other digital channels offer cost-effective tools for promoting products and services to a wider audience. Example: A large financial institutions in India launched a new online lending platform within 3 months using the cloud, allowing them to reach a wider audience through targeted digital marketing campaigns. Place: Cloud-based infrastructure enables remote access and collaboration, leading to increased efficiency and improved customer service across locations. NBFCs can expand their network and touchpoints more readily through cloud-based solutions, making them accessible to a broader customer base. Example: NBFCs like BharatPe leverage cloud-based platforms to offer mobile banking services, reaching customers in remote areas and expanding their reach beyond physical branch networks.

Conclusion: Cloud Economics serves as a powerful tool for digital NBFCs to achieve their business goals and unlock significant value. By embracing Cloud Economics principles, NBFCs can optimize their cloud investments, achieve cost savings, enhance operational efficiency, improve customer experience, and drive innovation. This, in turn, will help them stay competitive and thrive in the evolving Indian financial landscape.

11. The Impact of Human Resources Development on the Management of Organizational Crises in the Retail Industry: A Case Study of Malaysia.

Dejendran Rajendran

Lincoln University College **Malaysia**

Abstract: **T**his research explores the intricate relationship between human resources development (HRD) practices and crisis management within the retail industry of Malaysia. The retail sector, a vital contributor to Malaysia's economy, faces various challenges that can escalate into crises, jeopardizing organizational performance and reputation. While existing literature underscores the importance of crisis management strategies, the role of HRD in mitigating the impact of crises remains underexplored, particularly within the Malaysian retail context. This study adopts a mixed-methods approach, encompassing quantitative surveys and qualitative interviews, to investigate the impact of HRD on crisis management outcomes. The research aims to identify HRD practices implemented by retail organizations, analyze the types and frequency of crises experienced, examine the relationship between HRD practices and crisis management effectiveness, and explore the role of HRD in enhancing organizational resilience. The findings of this study hold significant theoretical and practical implications, informing policymakers, industry practitioners, and HR professionals about the importance of investing in HRD initiatives to mitigate the impact of crises and sustain organizational performance in the dynamic retail landscape of Malaysia.

Keywords: human resources development, crisis management, retail industry, Malaysia, organizational resilience, crisis preparedness.

Introduction

The retail industry is a significant contributor to Malaysia's economy, playing a crucial role in job creation and GDP growth. However, this sector is not immune to crises, which can range from economic downturns and supply chain disruptions to reputational threats and natural disasters. Effective crisis management is essential to navigate these challenges and sustain organizational performance. While much of the existing literature emphasizes the importance of crisis management strategies, the specific role of Human Resources Development (HRD) in mitigating the impact of crises is less explored, especially within the Malaysian retail context.

This study investigates the relationship between HRD practices and crisis management within the Malaysian retail industry. By adopting a mixed-methods approach, it aims to provide a comprehensive understanding of how HRD can enhance organizational resilience and crisis preparedness.

Literature Review: Crisis Management

Crisis management involves preparing for, responding to, and recovering from unexpected adverse events. Effective crisis management strategies are vital for minimizing the negative impact of crises on organizations. According to Hermann (1963), a crisis is an unexpected event that disrupts normal operations and requires immediate attention. Pearson and Clair (1998) emphasize the importance of developing crisis management plans that include communication strategies, leadership roles, and recovery procedures.

Human Resources Development: uman Resources Development (HRD) encompasses a range of practices aimed at improving employee skills, knowledge, and capabilities. These practices include training and development, career development, and organizational development (McLagan, 1989). HRD is critical for equipping employees with the skills needed to respond to and recover from crises, thus enhancing organizational resilience. Lengnick-Hall et al. (2011) argue that strategic HRD can foster a capacity for resilience by promoting continuous learning and adaptability.

Intersection of HRD and Crisis Management: While some studies suggest that HRD can contribute to organizational resilience, there is a lack of empirical research examining how HRD practices specifically impact crisis management outcomes in the retail industry, particularly in Malaysia. This study aims to fill this gap by exploring the role of HRD in mitigating the impact of crises and enhancing crisis preparedness.

Methodology: This study adopts a mixed-methods approach to investigate the impact of HRD on crisis management in the Malaysian retail industry. The research involves both quantitative surveys and qualitative interviews.

Quantitative Component: The quantitative component involves a survey distributed to HR professionals and managers within the Malaysian retail sector. The survey aims to identify the HRD practices implemented by these organizations, the types and frequency of crises experienced, and the perceived effectiveness of crisis management efforts. The survey includes questions on: Types of HRD practices (e.g., training programs, leadership development, career development) Frequency and types of crises (e.g., supply chain disruptions, economic downturns, reputational threats) Effectiveness of crisis management strategies Perceived impact of HRD practices on crisis management outcomes

Qualitative Component: The qualitative component includes in-depth interviews with HR professionals and managers. These interviews aim to explore the relationship between HRD practices and crisis management effectiveness, and to understand how HRD can enhance organizational resilience. Interview questions focus on:

- Specific HRD initiatives and their implementation

- Experiences with crisis situations and response strategies

- Perceptions of how HRD contributes to crisis preparedness and resilience

- Examples of successful HRD interventions during crises

Results

HRD Practices in the Retail Sector: The survey results indicate that Malaysian retail organizations implement a variety of HRD practices, including regular training programs, leadership development initiatives, and career development plans. These practices are aimed at improving employee competencies and preparing them for potential crises. For instance, some organizations have established continuous training programs that focus on crisis response and recovery, ensuring that employees are equipped with the necessary skills and knowledge to handle unexpected events.

Types and Frequency of Crises: he retail organizations reported experiencing various types of crises, including supply chain disruptions, economic downturns, and reputational threats. The frequency of these crises varies, with some organizations facing multiple crises annually. The data suggests that economic downturns and supply chain disruptions are the most common types of crises faced by the retail sector in Malaysia. These crises can significantly impact organizational performance and necessitate effective management strategies.

Relationship Between HRD and Crisis Management: The analysis reveals a positive relationship between HRD practices and crisis management effectiveness. Organizations that invest in comprehensive HRD programs are better equipped to handle crises and recover more quickly. These organizations report higher levels of employee preparedness and confidence in dealing with crisis situations. For example, retail organizations that provide regular crisis management training report that their employees feel more confident and capable of responding to crises effectively.

Enhancing Organizational Resilience: The qualitative interviews highlight the role of HRD in enhancing organizational resilience. HRD practices such as scenario-based training, leadership development, and team-building exercises help employees develop the skills and mindset needed to navigate crises effectively. Furthermore, these practices foster a culture of continuous learning and adaptability, which is crucial for organizational resilience. Interviewees emphasized that HRD initiatives have helped create a more agile and responsive workforce, capable of handling unexpected challenges.

Discussion

The findings of this study underscore the importance of HRD in managing organizational crises. By investing in HRD initiatives, retail organizations can enhance their crisis preparedness and resilience. This is particularly relevant in the dynamic retail landscape of Malaysia, where organizations must navigate various challenges to sustain performance.

Theoretical Implications: The study contributes to the existing body of knowledge by highlighting the significant role of HRD in crisis management. It provides empirical evidence that HRD practices can enhance crisis preparedness and resilience, thus supporting the theoretical proposition that HRD is a critical component of effective crisis management (Lengnick-Hall et al., 2011).

Practical Implications: For policymakers, the study highlights the need to support HRD initiatives within the retail sector to enhance overall economic resilience. For industry practitioners and HR professionals, the findings emphasize the importance of integrating HRD practices into crisis management strategies. Retail organizations should consider investing in comprehensive HRD programs that include crisis management training, leadership development, and team-building exercises to enhance their crisis preparedness and resilience.

Conclusion

This research provides valuable insights into the relationship between HRD and crisis management in the Malaysian retail industry. By identifying and analyzing the HRD practices that contribute to effective crisis management, this study offers a framework for enhancing organizational resilience. The findings suggest that retail organizations can benefit significantly from investing in HRD initiatives, as these practices enhance their ability to respond to and recover from crises.

Future Research

Future research should continue to explore the intersection between HRD and crisis management, particularly in other sectors and geographical contexts. Longitudinal studies could provide further insights into the long-term impact of HRD practices on organizational resilience and crisis management outcomes.

References

1. Hermann, C. F. (1963). Some consequences of crisis which limit the viability of organizations. *Administrative Science Quarterly*, 8(1), 61-82.

2. Lengnick-Hall, C. A., Beck, T. E., & Lengnick-Hall, M. L. (2011). Developing a capacity for organizational resilience through strategic human resource management. *Human Resource Management Review*, 21(3), 243-255.

3. McLagan, P. A. (1989). *Models for HRD practice*. American Society for Training and Development.

4. Pearson, C. M., & Clair, J. A. (1998). Reframing crisis management. *Academy of Management Review*, 23(1), 59-76.

12. Correcting Ethnocentrism By Acquiring Intercultural Communication Competence.

Natka Jankova Alagjozovska

PhD, Assistant professor at Goce Delcev University Stip, Faculty of Philology

Abstract: Intercultural communication is a field of culture coined by Hall in 1959 and nowadays is becoming an essential part of the education system because of globalization, immigration and the multicultural work environments. More training, knowledge and research in this field is essential because of the recent trends in education and other branches too. Intercultural communication is the type of communication that takes place within members of different cultures and aims to understand the cultural values, beliefs and norms of other parties. The only way to achieve successful communication with the other is only by understanding and accepting the differences between cultures. Ethnocentrism is another issue connected to intercultural communication. It is a notion that appears within cultures and one who is ethnocentric believes that their own culture is superior to other cultures and these beliefs very often lead to inaccurate judgements about other people and rely on stereotypes. However, good intercultural training focuses on avoiding stereotypes and learning how to develop intercultural awareness. A very important model in this field is the Bennett's model also called Developmental Model of Intercultural Sensitivity. This model implies that individuals with intercultural sensitivity tend to transform themselves from the ethnocentric stage to the ethno-relative stage. Bennett's model known as the Developmental Model of Intercultural Sensitivity (DMIS) consists of a continuum of six stages moving from "ethnocentrism" to "ethnorelativism" and can be a very useful model in the help of correcting ethnocentrism. This paper will reveal the secrets of correcting ethnocentrism by acquiring intercultural communication competence.

Keywords: culture, differences, intercultural communication, ethnocentrism, ethnorelativism.

Defining Intercultural Communication

In today's digitalized world which is global, Intercultural communication is something that is inevitable. However, it is a complex term and must explored from different perspectives in order to define and understand it. First, it is important to explore the terms culture and communication which are in relation to intercultural communication. There are numerous definitions of culture amongst which a very interesting one is by Tylor who wrote it in 1871 stating that culture is "that complex whole which includes knowledge, beliefs, arts, morals, law, customs and any other capabilities and habits acquired by a human as a member of society (p.2)". It is difficult to define culture and it is not strange that this word has also been described as one of the two or three most complicated words in English language. A very famous scholar in this field Hofstede (2001) defined it as "the collective mental programming or the software of the mind that distinguishes the members of one group or category of people from others" (p.9). However in his book Culture's Consequences (1980) he introduces the use of the concept of dimensions of culture: basic problems to which different national societies have over time developed different answers. National culture is what distinguishes one country from another. It is what every individual belonging to that culture is indoctrinated with. In one of his interviews, Hofstede makes the claim that the acquisition of one's national culture is an unconscious process, because we are born into a certain culture and by the age of 9 or 10 we have already acquired all of the elements, language, behaviors, values, history and organizations of that culture (October 10, 2011). This is done subconsciously, simply because that particular culture is the only culture we know and are exposed to. Consequently, one is so thoroughly imbued with all of the elements typical of their own culture that while growing up it becomes almost impossible to comprehend how anyone else's culture could be any different from theirs. The second level of culture defined by Hofstede is the culture we encounter as part of the working world i.e. organizational culture. The definition of this cultural subtype can be embedded in Hofstede's definition of national culture by simply replacing the terms group or category of people with organization, i.e. "the collective programming of the mind that distinguishes the members of one ... [organization] from others" (Hofstede, p. 9). The reason why culture is something that one should be aware of is that people need something to rely on. Everyone needs some moral and legal rules to follow and obey in order to know whether what is being done is right or wrong. Culture is what makes people feel as being part of something, and this is an inevitable desire of every human being. People want to know that they are a part of something and that there are other people who share their views, opinions and experiences. Culture and intercultural communication are inevitably connected. Culture gives essential information to communication. This brings understanding through a common background of mutual experiences, histories and geographical location. Shared experiences over the years and centuries create culture which is essential for understanding and communication. As Helen Spencer Oatey points out "the shared assumptions of a group of people help to interpret the behavior and words of those in and outside the group" (2012, p.2). She explores the interactive accepts of cross-cultural communication. Cross-cultural communication is not the same as intercultural communication. On the one hand, cross-cultural communication is not about the communication of people from different cultures but the comparison of their differences across culture. This means that cross-cultural communication is comparative in nature and deals with the communication patterns of different cultures. On the other hand, intercultural communication examines how the specific cultural differences affect the interactions of the people involved in that communication (Gudykunst, 2002).

Intercultural Communication Concepts: Intercultural communication competence means the ability to communicate in an effective and appropriate way with people from different cultures. In order to achieve appropriate and effective communication, one must value rules, norms of the other culture which can be fulfilled by having a more developed sense for intercultural communication. Intercultural communication cognition of English language teachers would mean the ability of teachers to incorporate intercultural communication knowledge, attitudes and awareness towards other cultures. Chen and Starosta (1999) define intercultural communication competence as "the ability to effectively and appropriately execute communication behaviors that negotiate each other's cultural identity or identities in a culturally diverse environment" (p. 28). They outline three key components of intercultural communication competence: intercultural sensitivity, intercultural awareness and intercultural adroitness defined as verbal and nonverbal skills needed to act effectively in intercultural interactions. In order to go into details of ICC, three models are to be explained in details below:

a)Process Model (D. Deardorff)

D. Deardorff's model of ICC is named Process Model of ICC. This model explains the process of how to become interculturally competent. This scholar has made a national study in the USA and concluded that ICC can be defined as effective and appropriate behavior and communication in intercultural situations. The main elements needed to achieve ICC are attitudes, knowledge, skills, internal or external outcomes. If attitude means the way you feel or think about someone and one of the key attitudes are respect, openness, curiosity and discovery these are needed to move further for successful intercultural communication. Knowledge about culture and sociolinguistic awareness is also needed to achieve successful intercultural interaction. In connection to this are the skills to process the knowledge such as observation, listening, analyzing and interpreting. All these lead to the internal outcome which includes flexibility, adaptability and empathy. Finally, empathy plays an important role for achieving the wanted external outcomes i.e. do not do to others what you do not want to be done and vice versa. From here the definition of ICC is the effective and appropriate behavior and communication in intercultural situations. Furthermore, Deardorff

(2006) suggests that this model is open and allows individuals to enter at any point and they can move freely between categories, sometimes moving ahead, and at other times returning to delve deeper into a concept previously encountered: This model confirms that if an individual has the needed attitudes and the minimal appropriate behavior and communication it is possible to achieve the desired outcome. When the person possesses knowledge and skills, he/she will be more effective in the intercultural interaction. This model shows that ICC is not a finalized process. One cannot become completely interculturally competent because this is a lifelong process. However, language is not the only needed skill for ICC but it is only a bridge to move on and develop more and more skills and understand the others. b)Byram's model. Byram's model in ICC whose concept is in cordance with linguistic competence, sociolinguistic competence and discourse competence and adds detailed intercultural dimension in order to move away from the native speaker model of communication. (Han & Song, 176). It also combines knowledge, skills and discovery and interaction, intercultural attitudes and critical cultural awareness into a system of intercultural competence. Thus, the role of the language is to develop skills, attitudes and awareness of values just as much as it is to develop a knowledge of a particular culture or country (Byram, 2008). According to Byram's model as shown in Figure 2 above, intercultural competence is made of knowledge, skills and attitudes and all these are supplemented by five values: intercultural attitudes, knowledge, skills of interpreting and relating, skills of discovery and interaction, critical cultural awareness (Byram, 2002). Byram gives explanation of ICC consisting of interaction with the "other" using the one's native language or interpretation of documents that have been translated into one's native language. Hence ICC is about combining the ideas of self-awareness in the process of communication in a foreign language as a needed component to the intercultural case. *Bennet's model* A very important approach connected to this issue is Bennet's model of cultural competence. According to Bennet (1993), "Cultural competence is the process by which people learn to value and respond respectfully to people off all cultures." (p. 245), and it is important to acquire intercultural communication competence which has two prerequisites:

-intercultural communication awareness

-intercultural communication sensitivity

According to the Developmental Model of Intercultural Sensitivity individuals with intercultural sensitivity tend to transform themselves from the ethnocentric stage to the ethno-relative stage. Bennett's model known as the Developmental Model of Intercultural Sensitivity (DMIS) consists of a continuum of six stages moving from "ethnocentrism" to "ethnorelativism." The ethnocentric stages are denial, defense, and minimization. The ethnorelative stages are acceptance, adaptation, and integration. This model is organized in six levels identifying the cognitive orientations of individuals in understanding cultural difference. Each level describes the perception of the cultural difference which is connected to the experiences of other cultures. By identifying the certain cultural difference, predictions about behavior and attitudes can be easily made and education can be organized to facilitate development along the model. The figure shows how moving from "ethnocentrism" i.e. the feeling that your individual culture is central, towards "ethnorelativism" which means that the individual's culture has experienced the context of other cultures by acceptance, adaptation and integration. The six stages will be explained in details below:

i.Denial

This stage represents the lowest rate of openness for other cultures. In this stage the individual is not aware of the existence of the other culture and it is as a result of physical and social isolation from such differences. This kind of a person is the ultimate ethnocentric one and as such the state of mind of this person has a limited degree of contact with different cultures (Bennet, 1986). At some point they are even not aware that the other cultures exist, and their own vision of the world is not challenged to see other cultures as they are.

ii.Defense

In this stage the person perceives the different cultures as threatening by forming negative stereotypes and different types of discrimination such as race, gender as a form of denigration of a particular group of people. This phase strengthens the relationships between the members of a certain group and establish a 'boundary' between the two seemingly opposing categories. Sometimes it can be about cultural superiority assuming that one's own culture is better than any other according to some evolutionary projections. Or in the ultimate stage of defense it is about feeling that "the other cultures are quite simply inferior to ours, on a continuum of which we are the apogee" (Chodzkienė, 2014).

iii.Minimalization

The final stage of ethnocentrism is the last attempt to bury the differences and it is presumed that humans are governed by common principles that guide values and conducts in their surroundings.

Minimalization suggests that individuals disregard and/or trivialize differences by burying them under the 'weight of cultural similarities' (Bennett, 1986: 183). If people are in an intercultural situation at this stage, they will deem that a simple awareness for interaction will be needed for successful communication. Somehow this is still an ethnocentric view because for these individuals, differences are just some variations of different cultures. Between the stages of minimalization and acceptance there is a transition which is characterized by a new way of perceiving the different cultures as dynamic and fluid and not as static and rigid.

iv. Acceptance

At this stage people do not have the expected behavior for acceptance but they start to behave as such. More precisely, they begin to give values to other cultures and begin to be co-creators of their own reality (Berger & Luckman, 1967). People in this phase start to find a way to explore differences of other cultures and do not feel that they are threatening to them. They begin to accept that people can have their own cultural norms and rules different from theirs and they feel amusement in that. This stage can be taken as the stage of marking openness in the way they perceive the differences.

v. Adaptation

This stage is essential for the development of intercultural communication. The process of acceptance of different cultures is a process of changes in behavior and perception of the world and it is the heart of intercultural communication. The basic form of adaptation is empathy. Bennet defines it as a temporary change of the frame of reference where we perceive situations as if we were the other person. Adaptation comes after acceptance and it is a change of behavior in terms of empathizing with people from another cultures.

vi.Integration

This is the last stage of openness to other cultures. In this stage the multicultural person is a one who is constantly in the process of becoming an integral part of a culture. This is being developed only after certain periods of living in different locations whereas the person contacts with different cultures. According to Bennet (1986) "Integration indicates that individuals are able to become 'a part of and apart from a given cultural context" (p.186). In the last stage of Bennett's model, integration sees ethnorelativism exposed by the ability of the person to consciously consider different cultures and frames of reference at once, and sees individuals becoming truly multicultural: they are not bound to or identify with only one cultural identity.

Conclusion

To sum up, culture means the characteristics and knowledge of a particular group of people, defined by their language, religion, cuisine, social habits, music and arts from one hand. On the other hand, Intercultural communication is the communication that takes place people from different cultures. The importance of acquiring Intercultural Communication Competence is needed in order to improve the language and the quality of communication. What is more important is that one does not need to acquire the native speaker proficiency but rather to improve the reading, writing, speaking and listening skill and finally the cultural skill that traches learners to become diplomats. Finally, it can be concluded that for developing intercultural competence not only having and acquiring knowledge of intercultural communication is enough, but also a transformation of attitude and views of the world. In this case the transfer of knowledge is needed but it is not the most essential goal. If one does not feel the burden on their own skin experience is difficult to transfer. Learning and doing research in this field can really help in solving all the problems that are still present all around the world such as racism, discrimination, ethnocentrism even wars. Learning and studying can really help in overcoming these problems and people involved in education should do everything in making this world a more peaceful place for living.

References:

1.Bennett, M. J. (1986). A Developmental Approach to Training for Intercultural Sensitivity. International Journal of Intercultural Relations, 10(2):179-195.

2.Berger, P., & Luckmann, T. (1967). The Social Construction of Reality: A Treatise in the Sociology of Knowledge. Garden City, NY: Doubleday.

3.Byram, M. (1990). Language learners' perceptions of a foreign culture: The teacher's Role. (ED324961). ERIC. https://eric.ed.gov/?id=ED324961

4.Byram, M; Gribkova, B; Starkey, H; (2002) Developing the Intercultural Dimension in Language Teaching. Strasbourg: The Council of Europe.

5.Byram, Michael. (2008). From Foreign Language Education to Education for Intercultural Dimension in Language Teaching. Strasbourg: The Council of Europe

6.Chen, G.M. & Starosta, W. J (1996). Intercultural Communication Competence: A Synthesis. Communication Yearbook, Newcastle, UK. Chiao, J. Y., & Ambady, N. (2007). Cultural neuroscience: Parsing universality and diversity across levels of analysis. In S. Kitayama & D. Cohen (Eds.), Handbook of cultural psychology (pp. 237-254). New York, NY: Guilford Press

7.Chodzkienė, Loreta. (2014) What Every Student Should Know About Intercultural Communication. Vilnius University Institute of Foreign Languages. Vilnius.

8.Deardorff, D. K. (2006). The Identification and Assessment of Intercultural Competence as a Student Outcome of Internationalization at Institutions of Higher Education in the United States. Journal of Studies in International Education.

9.Feng, A., Byram, M., & Fleming, M. (2009, May 21). Becoming Interculturally Competent through Education and Training. Languages for Intercultural Communication and Education, 18. Multilingual Matters.

10. Gudykunst, W.B. & Mody, B. (2002). Handbook of international and intercultural communication. Sage.

11. Han, X., & Song, L. (2011). Teacher Cognition of Intercultural Communicative Competence in the Chinese ELT Context. Intercultural Communication Studies, 20, 175-192.

12. Hofstede, Geert (2001). Culture's Consequences Comparing Values, Behaviors, Institutions and Organizations across Nations. Thousand Oaks, California: Sage Publications, Inc.

13. Hofstede. G. J. (Producer). (2011, October 10). Geert Hofstede on Culture. Podcast retrieved from http://www.youtube.com/watch?v=wdh40kgyYOY

14. Krashen, S. (1988). The Input Hypothesis: Issues and Implications. Harlow: Longman.

15. Spencer-Oatey, H. (2012). What is culture? A compilation of quotations. Global PAD Core Concepts. Retrieved from http://www2.warwick.ac.uk/fac/soc/al/globalpad/interculturalskills/

13. Digital Diasporas: Identity and Community in Online Literary Spaces.

Surajkumar H Chavan

Ph.D. Scholar - Karnatak University Dharwad, India

Abstract: The digital age has profoundly transformed how diasporic communities maintain cultural connections and negotiate identities. This paper explores the concept of digital diasporas, focusing on how online spaces such as forums, social media, and digital storytelling platforms facilitate new forms of community and identity. By analyzing interactions within these platforms, the study reveals how digital environments serve as modern communal spaces for discussing politics and policies, sharing experiences, and shaping cultural identities. The findings illustrate that forums enable deep, analytical discussions about diasporic experiences, social media foster dynamic and supportive communities, and digital storytelling platforms democratize publishing, allowing diasporic writers to connect with global audiences. Additionally, the research highlights the significant political influence exerted by diasporic communities through these digital platforms. By engaging in political discourse, mobilizing for social causes, and advocating for policy changes, diasporic communities leverage their digital presence to influence political and societal structures both in their host countries and their countries of origin. These digital platforms not only provide continuity and community for dispersed individuals but also empower diasporic communities to assert their cultural identities and participate actively in global political conversations, sometimes with dismay from native residents accusing diaspora of being unaware of ground situation causing discomfort to them. This research underscores the transformative potential of digital technologies in reshaping diasporic experiences and suggests directions for future studies on the intersection of literature, technology, diaspora, and political engagement.

Keywords: Digital Diaspora, Culture, Identity, Politics, Social media.

Introduction

In contemporary times, the concept of diaspora has broadened significantly beyond its historical roots. Originally, the term described the dispersion of Jews beyond Israel, but today it encompasses any community living outside their ancestral homelands while maintaining connections to them. Modern diasporas are formed through both voluntary and involuntary migration, including economic migrants, refugees, expatriates, and transnational communities. William Safran puts it as "Diaspora is now deployed as a metaphoric designation to describe expellees, political refugees, alien residents, immigrants and ethnic and racial minorities tout court" (85) This expanded definition reflects the diverse and multifaceted nature of global migration patterns in the 21st century. Modern diasporas play a significant role in the economies of both their home and host countries. Remittances sent back home are a vital source of income for many developing nations, supporting families and local economies. Additionally, diaspora entrepreneurs often invest in businesses and development projects in their countries of origin, creating economic opportunities and fostering growth. Politically, diaspora communities are increasingly active, engaging in lobbying, advocacy, and voting in their home countries' elections. They also influence policy decisions in their host countries, advocating for the rights and interests of their Despite their contributions, diaspora communities face several challenges. Balancing integration into host societies while preserving cultural identity can be difficult, often leading to issues of identity and belonging. Many diaspora members encounter discrimination and xenophobia, which can hinder their social and economic integration. Economic vulnerability is another concern, as migrants may face underemployment and exploitation. Moreover, managing transnational relationships and responsibilities can create stress and logistical difficulties. However, the resilience and adaptability of diaspora communities also present opportunities for cultural enrichment, economic development, and political influence in an increasingly interconnected world.Diaspora communities often emphasize the preservation of their cultural heritage and identity, which can be seen in their social and communal activities. This preservation manifests in various ways, such as maintaining native languages, celebrating traditional holidays, and establishing cultural centers and religious institutions. This strong sense of identity and connection to the homeland can persist over generations, creating a sustained link between the diaspora and their ancestral land. The historical context of diaspora usually implies a long-term, sometimes multi-generational, presence in host countries, often stemming from significant historical events such as colonization, slavery, or political conflict that led to large-scale dispersal.Digital connectivity has profoundly transformed the lives and experiences of diaspora communities worldwide. The connectivity becomes multi-faceted and widely connected both at macro and micro level. The study becomes difficult to overview the minute characteristics of such connections. Donya Alinejad et al.. in their study 'Diaspora and Mapping Methodologies: Tracing Transnational Digital Connections with 'Mattering Maps' did quantified study on diasporic experience and traced communication of female migrants from Turkey, Somalia and Romania who have settled in major European cities (London, Amsterdam and Rome) and their engagement in 'diasporic digitality'. The study emphasizes on the continuity with which diaspora involve themselves in digital sphere, especially in the issue specific discussions. But it also points out micro level and subjective difference in the digital sphere. In the current study the focus is on diaspora expression in the digital sphere. The focus groups are Forums, Social Media and Online Literary Spaces. This is a qualitative analysis on the literature and major theme of involvement. The analysis is based on popular forums, social media and literary sites and the recurring concepts discussed by the diaspora. The advent of the internet, social media, and mobile technologies has enabled diaspora members to maintain strong ties with their homelands, facilitating constant and instantaneous communication. This digital revolution allows diaspora communities to share cultural practices, traditions, and news, thereby preserving their cultural identities despite geographical distances. For instance, through platforms like Facebook, WhatsApp, and YouTube, diaspora members participate in cultural festivals, religious ceremonies, and family gatherings virtually. These digital interactions help sustain a sense of community and belonging among dispersed populations, reinforcing their connections to their cultural roots.Moreover, digital connectivity has empowered diaspora communities economically. It has enabled entrepreneurs to create and manage transnational businesses, fostering economic links between their host and home countries. Online marketplaces and digital payment systems facilitate the flow of remittances, which are crucial for the economies of many developing nations. Digital platforms provide diaspora members with access to global job markets and educational opportunities, enhancing their economic prospects. Politically, digital connectivity has given diaspora communities a more significant voice in both their host and home countries. Social media platforms and online forums allow diaspora members to engage in political discussions, advocate for their rights, and mobilize support for various causes. They can participate in campaigns, vote in elections, and influence policy decisions remotely. This political engagement is evident in various diaspora movements that have successfully lobbied for changes in immigration policies, human rights issues, and development initiatives in their home countries. The Arab Spring, for instance, saw significant involvement from diaspora communities who used social media to raise awareness and coordinate actions.However, digital connectivity also presents challenges for diaspora communities. The constant exposure to multiple cultural influences lead to identity conflicts, as individuals navigate their loyalties and affiliations between their host and home countries. Furthermore, the digital divide can exacerbate inequalities within diaspora communities, as not all members have equal access to technology and the internet. This disparity limit the benefits of digital connectivity for some individuals, creating gaps in communication, economic opportunities, and political engagement. The spread of misinformation and the potential for online surveillance pose risks to the privacy and security of diaspora, particularly those involved in political activism.Digital connectivity has had a profound impact on the identities of diaspora communities, fundamentally transforming how these identities are constructed, maintained, and expressed. The advent of the internet and social media has provided diaspora members with unprecedented access to their cultural heritage and home country, enabling them to engage with their cultural identity in ways that were previously impossible.One significant aspect of digital connectivity is its role in the hybridization of identity. Diaspora members are constantly exposed to both their native culture and the culture of their host country through digital platforms. This exposure leads to the creation of hybrid identities, where individuals blend elements of both cultures in their daily lives. For instance, a second-generation immigrant might incorporate traditional music and cuisine from their parents' homeland while also embracing the popular culture of their host country. This blending of cultures enriches the individual's identity, making it more complex and multifaceted. Digital connectivity thus fosters a dynamic interplay between preserving cultural heritage and adapting to new cultural contexts. Digital platforms enable diaspora communities to form and join virtual groups that are centered around shared identities and experiences. These online communities provide a space for diaspora members to discuss issues related to their cultural identity, share personal stories, and offer support to one another. This virtual solidarity helps individuals navigate the challenges of living in a foreign country, such as discrimination or cultural assimilation pressures. By connecting with others who share similar backgrounds and experiences, diaspora members can find a sense of community and validation for their cultural identity. These online interactions play a crucial role in strengthening and sustaining a collective identity among dispersed individuals. Digital connectivity has significantly influenced the identities of diaspora communities by enabling continuous engagement with cultural heritage, hybrid identities, and facilitating virtual communities. While it offers opportunities for cultural preservation and identity reinforcement, it also poses challenges such as identity conflicts and digital inequalities. Understanding the complex impact of digital connectivity on diaspora identity is essential for supporting the diverse and evolving identities of diaspora individuals in the modern world. As digital technologies continue to advance, their role in shaping diaspora identities will likely become even more significant.

Diaspora experience in Forums

A diaspora experience in forums vary greatly depending on the specific forum in question and the individual's background and identity as part of the diaspora community. Some common themes in diaspora experiences in forums include: Seeking connection and community: Diaspora individuals turn to forums as a way to connect with others from their home country or cultural background, to share experiences and resources, and to feel less isolated in their new or diasporic environment.Navigating identity and belonging: Diaspora individuals use forums as a space to explore and negotiate their identities, to seek advice on cultural or identity-related issues, and to find solidarity with others who share similar experiences of displacement and belonging. Addressing discrimination and stereotypes: Diaspora individuals use forums as a platform to challenge stereotypes, misinformation, and discrimination they may face in their new or host country, and to advocate for more accurate and diverse representations of their community. Sharing resources and information: Diaspora use forums as a way to exchange information, recommendations, and resources related to their culture, language, traditions, and community events. Discussions usually occur in linear way, for example, in the website https://www.indiandiaspora.org/discussion-forum individuals involve in connecting with other diaspora in order to tackle the alienation and gain resources and information. The information helps them in tackling day to day problem they face due to strangeness of the host country.On the other hand, forums such as Indiaspora.org, Africadiaspora.org, adf.org.za, ideaspora.org etc., provide a platform where the community is built to listen and guide the diasporic population. These platforms help in bringing together dispersed diaspora and they arrange various conferences and discussion events where prominent problems of diaspora are discussed. Also, such conferences provide systemic guide to diaspora to overcome challenges such as employment, what to do when they are discriminated, housing problems, and even simple things such as finding their native markets, food guide, child/elderly care and so on. The rich experience of senior diaspora bridges the gap of problems faced by young diaspora. Jennifer M. Brinkerhoff in her book *Digital Diasporas* details on the diaspora presence and expression in the digital sphere. She notes on her study on forums,The sites often provide opportunities to link dispersed diasporans beyond the adhoc connections made through discussion forums. For example, dating and matchmaking services may be available. Through online discussions members may provide referrals to other members for their own socioeconomic opportunities and advancement, and they may discuss and share information and referrals pertinent to helping the homeland. (48) aHer study emphasizes on the rigorous connectivity that are used in the structure of diaspora. Another efficient usage of such forums is to tackle identity issues of diaspore. The emigrants of under-developed and developing countries to developed countries face inhibitions due to language constraint and self-doubt. The experiences shared by the other older diaspora helps them in reassurance of their abilities. Such forums provide them confidence in building their own image and space in host nation. Identity loss that is faced by the diaspora is recurring topic in such forums. This is not only a concern to new diaspora even the second or third generation of diaspora face such issues. Diaspora feel pressure to assimilate to the dominant culture of their host country in order to fit in and succeed in their new environment. This results in the suppression or abandonment of their original cultural practices, language, and traditions. Being separated from their homeland and community lead to feelings of disconnection and alienation from their cultural roots, especially if they are unable to maintain strong ties with their cultural heritage through language, customs, and traditions.Diaspora face discrimination and marginalization in their new environment, which lead to a loss of pride and confidence in their cultural identity, as well as a desire to distance themselves from their heritage in order to avoid further discrimination. Second and third-generation diaspora experience a dilution of their cultural identity as they become more integrated into the mainstream culture of their host country and less connected to the traditions and values of their ancestors.Addressing identity loss in diaspora communities requires a recognition of the importance of cultural heritage, the promotion of cultural pride and appreciation, and the creation of spaces and resources for diaspora individuals to connect with and preserve their cultural identities. This is done through community events, language classes, cultural exchanges, and other initiatives that foster a sense of belonging and connection to one's roots. And forums provide such a platform where the diaspora find a connection with their cultural heritage. They are reassured that maintaining identity of their origin nation and culture does not hamper their prospect in host nation. The community gatherings arranged with such forums provide them a chance to participate in events that align with their identity.In contrary some forums also advocate for the free assimilation of the diaspora with host country identity. Even cultural and religious identity if one wants to incorporate from host country, these forums provide support to such groups as well. The global concept of identity is ever changing and diaspora are easily exposed to the vulnerabilities of such changes. Brinkerhoff further dwells into this identity formation,Rather than following a linear path, with subsequent generations following a predictable pattern, diasporans are likely to assume a hybrid identity leaning in one or the other direction based on the opportunities that identity may afford to them. (51)These forums are guiding such diaspora in establishing their identity however they want and see fit. Forums are becoming critical in assimilating these factors into their key themes. Especially in cultural and socio identity formation the dissemination of information becomes critical **Diaspora experience in Social Media:** The diaspora experience on social media is deeply influenced by how individuals and communities maintain cultural identity, navigate belonging, and foster connections across geographical boundaries. Social media platforms such as Facebook,

Instagram, Twitter, Reddit and specialized forums play crucial roles in shaping these experiences by providing spaces for engagement, expression, and community-building. One of the primary ways social media impacts the diaspora experience is through the preservation and transmission of cultural heritage. Diaspora communities use these platforms to share traditions, languages, and customs with both their immediate family members and broader community. This digital sharing helps to keep cultural practices alive, particularly among younger generations who might be geographically distant from their ancestral homes. Platforms like YouTube and TikTok have become popular for sharing cultural content, ranging from cooking traditional recipes to performing cultural dances, thereby fostering a sense of identity and continuity. Common mode of connect on social media is through groups or pages in sites like Facebook and Instagram. On X(Former Twitter) and Threads many handles and specially hashtags provide the connectivity for the people to connect. Sites like Reddit and Discord provide anonymous connectivity for burning topics to be discussed. Apps like Snapchat provide more robust connectivity among younger generation. Other sites like LinkedIn provide professional connectivity for the diaspora which helps them in growing their professional presence. All these social media platforms enable diaspora to stay connected with their homeland. Through news updates, live streams, and direct communication with family and friends, individuals remain informed and involved in the socio-political landscapes of their countries of origin (Alonso & Oiarzabal, 2010;

Alunni, 2019). This connectivity is vital during times of political upheaval or natural disasters, as it allows for real-time information sharing and mobilization of support. Especially during wars social media is essential in guiding the diaspora to safety. Another significant aspect is the creation of virtual communities that offer support and solidarity. Diaspora often face challenges such as cultural assimilation, discrimination, and identity struggles. Just like forums social media provide safe spaces where they can share experiences, seek advice, and find emotional support. Anas Ansar & Abu Faisal Md. Khaled in their study of Rohingya migration examine the social media usage in such migration, In digital migration studies, research has made a significant contribution to understanding refugees' engagement with social media and other digital tools to stay in contact with transnational families during their migration (3)Social media becomes more efficient for real time dissemination of information and also helps to find immediate support from the local and native participants. These virtual communities are instrumental in helping individuals navigate the complexities of living between cultures and managing dual identities.Social media has given rise to transnational activism among diaspora communities. These platforms enable the organization and coordination of social and political movements, allowing diasporic individuals to advocate for causes related to their homelands (Gerbaudo P. and Treré E. 2015) For instance, hashtags and online campaigns have been pivotal in raising awareness and mobilizing resources for various issues, from human rights abuses to environmental crises. In addition to these benefits, social media also presents challenges for diaspora communities. The representation of cultural stereotypes, misinformation, and cyberbullying are issues that many face online. Balancing the authentic portrayal of one's culture while countering negative stereotypes requires careful navigation and resilience.

The Diaspora Experience in Literary Spaces: The diaspora experience in literary spaces such as self-publication, Quora, blogs, and Medium offers a unique and powerful avenue for expression, storytelling, and community engagement. These platforms provide individuals from diaspora communities with opportunities to share their narratives, cultural lineage, and contribute to broader conversations about identity, belonging, and migration. Self-publication has revolutionized the way diaspora authors share their stories. Traditional publishing often comes with barriers, including gatekeeping and a lack of representation for diverse voices. Self-publication platforms such as Amazon Kindle Direct Publishing, Smashwords, and Lulu allow diaspora writers to bypass these barriers and publish their works independently. This democratization of publishing has led to an increase in the availability of literature that reflects the diverse experiences of diaspora communities, offering authentic stories that otherwise remain untold. Authors explore themes of displacement, cultural identity, and the immigrant experience, reaching a global audience without the constraints imposed by traditional publishing houses. Quora, a popular question-and-answer platform, enables diaspora individuals to share their knowledge and experiences with a curious global audience. On Quora, users ask questions about cultural practices, migration experiences, and identity issues, and receive detailed, personal responses from those who have lived these experiences. This interactive platform fosters a sense of community and understanding, as people from various backgrounds engage in meaningful dialogue and share their perspectives. Diaspora often use Quora to dispel myths, provide insights into their cultures, and offer advice on navigating life in a new country. Moreover, diaspora communities influence the political landscape of their host countries. They often engage in local politics, voting in elections, running for office, and participating in civic activities. Their involvement lead to increased representation and attention to issues affecting immigrant communities, thereby shaping policy and public discourse. Despite the positive contributions of diaspora political engagement, there is often opposition from local populations. In home countries, some people view diaspora involvement with suspicion or resentment, perceiving them as outsiders who are disconnected from the daily realities on the ground. This disconnect can lead to accusations that diaspora groups are out of touch or are trying to impose their own agendas without fully understanding the local context. Additionally, political leaders in home countries may see influential diaspora groups as a threat to their power, leading to efforts to marginalize or discredit their activities. In host countries, opposition to diaspora political influence stem from concerns about loyalty and integration. Locals question the allegiance of diaspora communities, fearing that their involvement in homeland politics detracts from their commitment to the host country. There can also be tensions around issues such as immigration and multiculturalism, with some local populations feeling that diaspora communities are changing the cultural and political landscape in ways that are unwelcome. Furthermore, the political mobilization of diaspora groups can sometimes lead to polarization and conflict within host countries. For instance, if a diaspora group advocates for a controversial issue related to their homeland, it provoke backlash and deepen societal divisions. Host country governments may also face diplomatic challenges in balancing the interests of influential diaspora communities with broader foreign policy objectives.

Conclusion

The advent of digital technologies has significantly transformed the experiences of diaspora communities. Social media platforms, self-publication tools, blogs, and other online spaces have provided diasporic individuals with unprecedented opportunities to maintain cultural ties, express their identities, and engage in transnational political activism. These platforms enable the preservation and transmission of cultural heritage, the creation of virtual communities for support and solidarity, and the amplification of voices that might otherwise be marginalized in traditional media.Digital platforms have also democratized literary spaces, allowing diaspora writers to bypass traditional publishing barriers and reach global audiences with their narratives. This has enriched the literary landscape with diverse perspectives on migration, identity, and belonging. In the political realm, digitization has facilitated diaspora engagement through online campaigns, crowdfunding, and virtual meetings, enhancing their ability to influence political outcomes both in their host and home countries. Despite the challenges posed by digital media, such as misinformation and cultural stereotypes, the overall impact on diaspora communities is profoundly positive. The digital revolution has empowered diasporic individuals to connect, share, and advocate in ways that were previously unimaginable, fostering a more interconnected and dynamic global community.

References

1. Alonso A, Oiarzabal P. The immigrant worlds' digital harbors: an introduction. In: Alonso A, Oiarzabal PJ (eds.) Diasporas in the new media age: identity, politics, and community. University of Nevada Press, Nevada, 2010

2. Brinkerhoff, Jennifer M. *Digital Diasporas*. UK, Cambridge UP, 2009

3. Everett, Anna. *Digital Diaspora*. SUNY Press, 2009.

4. Gerbaudo P, Treré E. In search of the 'we' of social media activism: introduction to the special issue on social media and protest identities. Inf Commun Soc 18(8):865–871. https://doi.org/10.1080/1369118X.2015.1043319, 2015

5. Kapur D. *Diaspora, development, and democracy: the domestic impact of international migration from India.* Princeton University Press, New Jersey, 2010

6. Ponzanesi, S. Digital Diasporas: Postcoloniality, Media and Affect. *Interventions, 22*(8),   2020,   977–993. https://doi.org/10.1080/1369801X.2020.1718537

7. Sarkar, Sucharita. "Blogging Across Borders – Memories, Recipes and Identity in the Diaspora." *Problematics on Ethnicity, Identity and Literature: Pre-conference Proceeding Volume, ISEIL 2012,* Jan. 2015, pp. 851–58.

    www.academia.edu/5108171/Blogging_Across_Borders_Mem ories_Recipes_and_Identity_in_the_Diaspora.

8. William Safran, 'Diasporas in modern societies: myths of homeland and return', *Diaspora I*: I, 1991, p. 83.

14. Enhancing the Efficiency of RSA Cryptosystem with ChaCha20-Poly1305: A novel Hybrid Encryption Approach.

Paul K. Arhin Jnr[1], Prof. Frimpong Twum[2], Dr. Gaddafi A. Salaam[2] and Prof. George Aggrey[1]

[1]Department of Computer Science and I.T, University of Cape Coast, **Ghana**

[2]Department of Computer Science, Kwame Nkrumah University of Science and Technology, **Ghana**

Abstract: Although the RSA algorithm is well known for its strong security, it has serious computational efficiency issues, especially when encrypting huge amounts of data. This research work presents a novel hybrid encryption scheme, RSA-ChaPoly, that combines RSA and the ChaCha20-Poly1305 algorithm to overcome these constraints. Contemporary authenticated encryption algorithm ChaCha20-Poly1305 is renowned for its excellent security and performance. The suggested hybrid technique seeks to improve the overall efficiency and security of cryptographic operations by utilizing the secure key exchange capabilities of RSA and the speed and efficiency of ChaCha20-Poly1305 for data encryption. Performance benchmarks, security assessments, and the integration procedure are all thoroughly examined in this study. In comparison to conventional RSA implementations, the results show notable improvements in encryption and decryption rates, less computing overhead, and maintained or increased security levels. Applications like data storage, real-time systems, and secure communications that demand effective and safe encryption can benefit from this method.

Keywords: RSA, ChaCha20-Poly130, RSA-ChaPoly, Hybrid Encryption

Introduction

The RSA algorithm, which is well-known for its strong asymmetric encryption capabilities, is a backbone of secure communications in the field of modern cryptography [1][2]. But RSA still has a lot of issues with computing efficiency, especially when it comes to large-scale data encryption, even with its extensive use and established security [3][4]. Applications that require both security and performance are less likely to benefit from RSA operations due to their significant computational overhead and inherent mathematical complexity [5]. This constraint emphasises the necessity of developing novel strategies to increase RSA's effectiveness without compromising its security guarantees. This work suggests RSA-ChaPoly, a novel hybrid encryption system that combines RSA with the ChaChaPoly-1305 algorithm in a synergistic way, as a solution to this difficulty. The contemporary authenticated encryption method ChaChaPoly-1305 is commended for both its robust security features and excellent performance [6][7][8]. The suggested hybrid solution seeks to solve the computational inefficiencies of conventional RSA implementations by utilising the safe key exchange capabilities of RSA [9] and the speed and efficiency of ChaChaPoly-1305 for data encryption [10]. RSA is utilised in the RSA-ChaPoly hybrid method to safely exchange a symmetric key, which is subsequently used by ChaChaPoly-1305 to encrypt the data itself. This integration takes advantage of ChaChaPoly-1305's fast encryption and decryption operations while preserving the asymmetric encryption benefits of RSA for safe key distribution. The resulting system is intended to provide increased efficiency, especially in situations where there are few computational resources or where quick data processing is essential. This paper offers a thorough investigation of the hybrid encryption scheme that combines RSA with ChaPoly, including information on performance benchmarks, security assessments, and integration process. The research shows notable gains in encryption and decryption speeds, less computing cost, and strong security advantages over traditional RSA implementations through rigorous testing and comparative analysis. According to the results, RSA-ChaPoly offers a workable and practical solution for safe data storage, real-time encryption systems, and secure communications. This meets the urgent demand for effective cryptographic techniques in a world where data is becoming more and more important. The goal of this research is to continue developing cryptographic approaches that strike a balance between security and efficiency by pushing the field of hybrid encryption forward. Well-known cryptographic algorithms can be combined to develop novel solutions that adapt to the changing needs of contemporary cybersecurity, as demonstrated by the RSA-ChaPoly method. **RSA and ChaCha20-Poly1305 Hybrid Encryption Algorithm** RSA's strength in safe key exchange and ChaCha20-Poly1305's efficiency and security in data encryption are combined in the hybrid encryption technique known as RSA-ChaPoly. The steps in the algorithm are outlined in this section.

Generation of RSA Keys: RSA key pair (*RSA_public_key*, *RSA_private_key*) of different bit sizes (1024, 2048, 3071, 4096) is generated

Generating ChaCha20-Poly1305 Symmetric Key: Generate a 256-bit symmetric key (K_s). Generate a 96-bit nonce (N)

Using RSA to encrypt Symmetric Key: Encrypt the symmetric key (K_s) with the recipient's RSA public key (RSA_public_key) using OAEP padding: $E\_Ks = RSA\_encrypt\ (RSA\_public\_key,\ K\_s)$.

Using ChaCha20-Poly1305 to Encrypt Data: Encrypt plaintext P using K_s and N with ChaCha20-Poly1305. This will yield ciphertext C and authentication tag T

Encrypted Data packaged: Concatenate E_Ks, N, and C to form the final encrypted message M.

Using RSA to decrypt Symmetric Key: Extract E_Ks, N, and C from the received message M.

Decrypt E_Ks with the recipient's RSA private key (*RSA_private_key*) to obtain K_s. $K\_s = RSA\_decrypt\ (RSA\_private\_key,\ E\_Ks)$.

Using ChaCha20-Poly1305 to decrypt data: Decrypt C using K_s and N with ChaCha20-Poly1305 to recover plaintext P

Related Works: Dutta et al [11] in their paper, Enhancement of Mobile Ad Hoc Network Security Using Improved RSA Algorithm, combined DES with RSA for better performance. By integrating DES for more secure and reliable transmission with key lengths up to 2048 bits, the study suggests an improved RSA algorithm for mobile ad hoc networks, which can be applied to a variety of network types, including new generation networks. The suggested approach works well for small messages and can also be used to significantly improve data security in a variety of networks, including modern networks. DES was integrated with RSA for larger data volumes in order to provide better and more secure transmission. It was possible to achieve more secure and effective data transmission by merging DES and RSA. This work proposes a modified technique that incorporates multiple public keys, exponential powers, n prime numbers, and the K-NN algorithm, which improves upon the traditional RSA algorithm. Verification is another benefit that the modified technique offers both the sender and recipient [12]. In his paper [13], Sarjiyus presents an enhanced RSA cryptographic algorithm security by modifying the public key. In order to secure sensitive data during online transactions, the article addresses improving RSA security capabilities through public key modification, with an emphasis on quicker key generation and higher security levels. Systems that prioritize strong security over speed of execution can benefit from the modified RSA approach, which creates more complex ciphers during encryption. The findings demonstrate that the enhanced RSA technique, which is based on public key transformation, increased the security of the modified RSA by producing more complex ciphers throughout the encryption process than the current RSA technique. The enhanced RSA exhibits marginally higher time complexity during the encryption process, but not during decryption, in terms of performance. Thus, systems that require great security but low execution performance are best suited for the new RSA approach. Mezher [14] presented an enhanced RSA cryptosystem which is intended to strengthen security by using numerous public and private keys for encryption and decryption. In comparison to the conventional RSA algorithm, the enhanced algorithm showed to be more robust and stable against brute force attacks. At the use of different key sizes, the new algorithm was slower to break. In this paper [15], Mahajan et al covers the significance of cryptography in contemporary computer security, the necessity of improving the RSA algorithm's performance, the parallelization of GPU programming, and the outcomes of tests contrasting CPU and GPU RSA for both small and big prime numbers. The goal of the study is to use NVIDIA's CUDA platform to create GCD comparisons of RSA keys, which should speed up the RSA method. The paper tackles the RSA algorithm's underlying issues with speed and the usage of small or subpar prime numbers, which have resulted in serious security flaws. According to the results, the CUDA framework can improve execution performance. A paper presented by Abdulkader [16] compares RSA with CRT to standard RSA, highlights the dependence of RSA security on prime number factorization issues, highlights the significance of computer and network security, presents a modified RSA approach for secure data transmission, and concludes that the advanced RSA model with multiple keys is more secure. In order to improve performance metrics such as speed, throughput, power consumption, and the avalanche effect, Et.al [17] presents a modification of the RSA algorithm that uses the Euclidean technique. Experimental results confirm that the Euclidean-RSA algorithm performs better than the RSA algorithm with the GCD technique, and the results point to potential directions for future research to further improve the security and performance of RSA. The approach comprised altering the RSA algorithm with the Euclidean technique, assessing performance metrics with input file sizes varying from 226 to 289 bytes, and utilizing the GCD technique to compare the outcomes with the RSA algorithm. When comparing the RSA algorithm with the GCD technique to the Euclidean technique, several performance metrics were seen to have improved: encryption time; memory consumption; execution time; Avalanche effect; encryption; decryption; throughput; and power consumption.

Mustafi et al [18] propose a novel algorithm for enhancing the security aspect of the RSA algorithm and removing potential security risks by making using a two-variable bijective function to enhance security. In 2010, Hong-mei [19] presented a paper that compares and analyses the encryption algorithms used by DES and RSA, and it suggests a distributed system design for a data transmission system that will guarantee secure data transfer between agents and the central controller. This system can be used in a variety of application and has good operability. A thorough discussion was conducted by Purnima et al [20] in a paper that examines the use of cloud computing for data storage, evaluates different encryption algorithms, and suggests a way to employ multi-threading on multi-core CPUs to increase the speed of RSA encryption.

Methodology

The goal of this research is intended to illustrate the effectiveness of the hybrid encryption algorithm known as RSA-ChaPoly. This method fixes the computational inefficiencies of conventional RSA encryption while preserving its security benefits. It does this by fusing the strong security of RSA with the great performance of ChaChaPoly-1305. The methodical approach for designing, implementing, benchmarking, and analysing the RSA-ChaPoly algorithm is described, with an emphasis on three critical performance metrics: power consumption, memory usage, and encryption and decryption speed. To ensure that RSA and ChaChaPoly-1305 work together perfectly, the hybrid algorithm is first developed and implemented. In order to secure both RSA and ChaChaPoly-1305 keys, key creation and management procedures are defined. The strengths of both algorithms are then combined to offer improved performance and security in the encryption and decryption methods. The hybrid algorithm is developed using effective and safe programming techniques. Python programming language is utilised for development, taking advantage of its rich library support and readability. The PyCryptodome library is used to implement the RSA and ChaChaPoly-1305 cryptographic functions. Modular component integration makes testing and future improvements easier. An Intel Core i7-9700K processor with eight cores and a base clock of 3.6 GHz (up to 4.9 GHz with Turbo Boost), 32 GB of DDR4-2666 RAM, and a 1 TB NVMe SSD for storage will be used for development and testing. Ubuntu 20.04 LTS will be the operating system, and Python 3.8, the PyCryptodome module, and the required benchmarking tools will be included in the software environment. Performance testing is carried out in a controlled setting using typical datasets to assess the effectiveness of the algorithm with respect to power consumption, memory usage, and encryption and decryption performance. Next, a comparison with traditional RSA is conducted to show how the hybrid technique improves these important performance indicators. Together with qualitative and quantitative measurements, a comprehensive picture of RSA-ChaPoly's benefits is seen.

Result And Analysis

The results present a comparison of the time and space complexities between the conventional RSA algorithm and the hybrid RSA-ChaPoly approach, utilizing various key sizes and corresponding message sizes

Table 1: Comparing Time complexities (Encryption and Decryption speeds) of RSA and RSA-ChaPoly with different key sizes and corresponding message size

Key Size (Bits)	RSA Encryption Speed	RSA-ChaPoly Encryption Speed	RSA Decryption Speed	RSA-ChaPoly Decryption Speed

1024	45.2	4.8	63.1	6.5
2048	93.5	7.2	129.8	9.8
3072	141.9	9.1	193.2	12.3
4096	192.1	11.4	259.4	15.2

Table 1 shows a comparison between the time complexities (encryption and decryption speeds) of RSA and RSA-ChaPoly at different key sizes. It is evident from the table that RSA-ChaPoly outperforms traditional RSA in terms of encryption and decryption speeds for all key sizes. This demonstrates how the hybrid method increased efficiency As the key size increases, the performance difference between RSA and RSA-ChaPoly grows, suggesting that RSA-ChaPoly is more scalable and appropriate for settings where high key sizes are required for more security. In terms of encryption speed, the RSA-ChaPoly algorithm is roughly 13.7 times faster than the conventional RSA algorithm and 13.9 times faster in terms of decryption speed. This significant speed increase is made possible by utilising ChaChaPoly-1305's effective symmetric encryption and demonstrates the efficiency gains provided by the hybrid approach. Figure 2 shows the comparison of encryption and decryption speeds between RSA and RSA-ChaPoly for different key sizes. RSA's encryption time grows noticeably with increasing key size, however RSA-ChaPoly's remains relatively efficient. Similar to encryption, RSA-

ChaPoly retains a significantly lower decryption time while RSA's climbs noticeably with bigger key sizes.

Key Size (Bits)	RSA Encryption	RSA-ChaPoly Encryption	RSA Decryption	RSA-ChaPoly Decryption
1024	1.39	0.82	2.17	1.33
2048	2.85	1.35	4.19	1.77
3072	4.22	1.58	6.43	2.47
4096	5.71	2.15	8.34	3.03

Table 2: Comparison between the space complexity (memory consumption) of RSA and RSA-ChaPoly Table 2 shows the space complexity comparison of RSA and RSA-ChaPoly for different key sizes. The findings demonstrate that, in comparison to conventional RSA, RSA-ChaPoly consistently utilises less memory for both encryption and decryption. This analysis demonstrates how memory-efficient the hybrid RSA-ChaPoly algorithm is. When compared to regular RSA, RSA-ChaPoly consistently utilises less memory for both encryption and decryption, giving it a more memory-efficient option. While RSA-ChaPoly keeps a more controllable memory footprint, RSA's memory usage increases dramatically as key sizes rise. When it comes to memory usage for encryption, RSA-ChaPoly requires 58.36% less than conventional RSA. The hybrid algorithm's effectiveness in allocating memory resources during encryption is demonstrated by this notable decrease. When it comes to decryption, RSA-ChaPoly exhibits

a greater improvement with an average memory usage of 59.30% less than RSA, which makes it a highly effective substitute for RSA, particularly in settings where memory utilisation is a major concern.

Conclusion

When compared to the conventional RSA, the RSA-ChaPoly hybrid encryption algorithm exhibits distinct advantages in terms of time and space complexities. RSA-ChaPoly is a great option for contemporary cryptographic applications because of its notable increases in encryption and decryption speeds and notable decreases in memory use. The association between decreased memory consumption and increased time efficiency highlights how well ChaChaPoly-1305 and RSA work together to provide a well-balanced solution that satisfies security, performance, and resource management requirements.

References

[1]   Birrell, E. (2017). CS 5431 – Computer Security Practicum Spring 2017 Lecture 4: RSA in Practice February 17, 2017 Instructor

[2]   Nisha, S., & Farik, M. (2017). RSA Public Key Cryptography Algorithm – A Review. International Journal of Scientific & Technology Research, 6, 187-191.

[3]   Zhang, H., Yu, J., Tian, C., Tong, L., Lin, J., Ge, L., & Wang, H. (2020). Efficient and Secure Outsourcing Scheme for RSA Decryption in Internet of Things. IEEE Internet of Things Journal, 7, 6868-6881.

[4] Bhaskar, R.A., Hegde, G., & Vaya, P.R. (2012). An efficient hardware model for RSA Encryption system using Vedic mathematics. Procedia Engineering, 30, 124-128.

[5] Centeno, H.M., Meneses, F., Fuertes, W., Sancho, J., Salvador, S., Flores, D., Castro, F., Torres, J.G., Miranda, A., & Nuela, D. (2016). RSA encryption algorithm optimization to improve performance and security level of network messages.

[6] Feng, Y. (2024). Design of an Encryption Chat Application Based on ChaCha20-Poly1305. Highlights in Science, Engineering and Technology.

[7] Santis, F.D., Schauer, A., & Sigl, G. (2017). ChaCha20-Poly1305 authenticated encryption for high-speed embedded IoT applications. Design, Automation & Test in Europe Conference & Exhibition (DATE), 2017, 692-697.

[8] Serrano, R., Duran, C., Hoang, T., Sarmiento, M., Tsukamoto, A., Suzaki, K., & Pham, C. (2021). ChaCha20-Poly1305 Crypto Core Compatible with Transport Layer Security 1.3. 2021 18th International SoC Design Conference (ISOCC), 17-18.

[9] MacKenzie, P.D., Patel, S., & Swaminathan, R.P. (2000). Password-authenticated key exchange based on RSA. International Journal of Information Security, 9, 387-410.

[10] Wei, Y., Li, B., Zhang, B., Yan, Y., & Zhou, Q. (2023). High-performance Data Hybrid Encryption Scheme Based on Mimic Defense. 2023 3rd International Symposium on Computer Technology and Information Science (ISCTIS), 114-121.

[11]   Dutta, S.C., Singh, S., & Singh, V. (2015). Enhancement of Mobile Ad Hoc Network Security Using Improved RSA Algorithm. International Conference on Soft Computing for Problem Solving.

[12]   Mathur, S., Gupta, D., Goar, V.K., & Kuri, M. (2017). Analysis and design of enhanced RSA algorithm to improve the security. 2017 3rd International Conference on Computational Intelligence & Communication Technology (CICT), 1-5.

[13]   Sarjiyus, O. (2020). Enhancing RSA Security Capability Using Public Key Modification.

[14]   Mezher, A.E. (2018). Enhanced RSA Cryptosystem based on Multiplicity of Public and Private Keys. International Journal of Electrical and Computer Engineering (IJECE).

[15]   Mahajan, S., & Singh, M.P. (2014). Analysis of RSA algorithm using GPU programming. ArXiv, abs/1407.1465.

[16]   Abdulkader, H., Samir, R., & Hussien, R.M. (2019). Improved RSA security using Chinese Remainder Theorem and Multiple Keys. Future Computing and Informatics Journal.

[17] Et.al, R.F. (2021). Improvement of RSA Algorithm Using Euclidean Technique.

[18]   Mustafi, K., Sheikh, N.U., Hazra, T.K., Mazumder, M., Bhattacharya, I., & Chakraborty, A.K. (2016). A novel approach to enhance the security dimension of RSA algorithm using bijective function. 2016 IEEE 7th Annual Information

Technology, Electronics and Mobile Communication Conference (IEMCON), 1-6.

[19] Hong-mei, G. (2010). Design of DES and RSA-based Data Encryption Transmission System Design. Communications Technology.

[20] Gupta, P., Kumar Verma, D., & Kumar Singh, A. (2018). Improving RSA Algorithm Using Multi-Threading Model for Outsourced Data Security in Cloud Storage. 2018 8th International Conference on Cloud Computing, Data Science & Engineering (Confluence), 14-15.